MY NDTV DAYS

MY NDTV DAYS

Anecdotes from the Life of a Journalist

SANJAY PINTO

PAN

First published 2018 by Pan
an imprint of Pan Macmillan Publishing India,
Pan Macmillan India, 707, Kailash Building
26 K. G. Marg, New Delhi – 110 001
www.panmacmillan.co.in

Pan Macmillan, 20 New Wharf Road, London N1 9RR
Basingstoke and Oxford
Associated companies throughout the world
www.panmacmillan.com

ISBN 978-93-86215-59-8

1 3 5 7 9 8 6 4 2

Typeset by Manmohan Kumar
Printed and bound in India by
Replika Press Pvt. Ltd.

Dedicated To

My late Mother Judith Pinto, who would wake up even at 2 am to make breakfast for me whenever I had to rush out on shoots at odd hours.

My father A.V. Pinto, who inculcated the habit of writing a 'Report For The Day' during my formative school years.

My wife Vidya, who used to watch all my stories, even the repeats.

My precious twin angels - Sanvi & Vidan who put up with my long hours on the laptop on weekends.

Prannoy Roy & Radhika Roy for being role models, not bosses.

CONTENTS

PREFACE

24X7 TELEVISION JOURNALISTS ARE always a big hit at social gatherings. Breaking and gathering news, rubbing shoulders with celebrities or having run-ins with those in the corridors of power, guarantees not just a captive but also a captivated audience.

Being catapulted on the national Star News channel with an international footprint, straight from Law School, I must confess, was heady stuff. I was just 24, turbo-charged, well paid, with perks like a mobile phone, quite uncommon in the age of pagers in the late nineties, and didn't mind the pressure of seemingly impossible deadlines, long hours and off days that were 'never written in stone'.

NDTV's distinct 'first come' advantage, being the first private national English broadcaster, made many of us household names and recognisable faces across the country. Those were gentler times. The 9'O Clock News, initially anchored by the inimitable Prannoy Roy, was almost compulsive, appointment viewing. (As a school boy, I remember being glued to The World This Week.) There was no shouting or screaming on Prime time. In those half-hour bulletins, pan India stories from across India were aired. NDTV was the first news channel to allow Correspondents to own their reports with their own scripts, voiceovers and Pieces to Camera.

Over the years, and I believe, much to the detriment of television journalism, the 'breaking news' hysteria, the surround sound fuss through slanging matches that pass for debates, copy cat story leads and hashtag news have come to characterise the electronic media. I was lucky to have been a part of a saner period, even as I was also inevitably sucked into the quicksand of TRP driven content.

A burning desire to chronicle my happy times, the pride of belonging to a world class organisation, working alongside the biggest names in the industry, the excitement of chasing the news, the adventures, the lessons, the hits and misses, had been on my mind during the last few years of my 14-year innings with NDTV that ended in 2012. However, chronologically, I was a Public Speaker before becoming a TV journalist and a book on that art, justifiably overtook this one. My present avatar as a lawyer led to a compendium of my legal columns last year, making this my third book.

Recounting stories that were up to two decades old was not easy. My darling wife Vidya kept pushing me to keep writing chapters, as I juggled between my career as a lawyer, and my pastime of writing columns, appearing on TV debates and mentoring youngsters in public speaking, not to forget my profound grief over the loss of my beloved mother Judith Pinto last year and a string of illnesses in the family. I have run the extra mile to complete this book.

It is not meant to offend or stir up controversies. While it is fashionable to lambast the media today, my book highlights the challenges of news gathering. This may also help readers get an inkling of the stress of ball-by-ball field reporting under trying circumstances, that many of my former colleagues go through today. In many ways, it's also a thanksgiving to those who shaped my career in TV journalism. Just like my reports, I've tried to tell the story like it is.

For one last time, in Chennai, Sanjay Pinto, NDTV.

[illegible] the [illegible] to complete this book.

[illegible]

[illegible]

1

DOUBLE FAULT!

THE MAJESTIC STANCE, THE diving volley, the power-packed forehand and returns, the sheer athleticism: Boris Becker was poetry in motion at the court. As a schoolboy, I was in awe of his game.

When you are catapulted into the rough and tumble of television reporting straight from Law school, be prepared for baptism by fire. A champion at a press conference, especially after one of the biggest upsets in tennis history, is no witness on the stand to be cross-examined! A lesson I learnt the hard way. The transition from a diehard fan to a hardnosed critic was as bumpy as the pothole-ridden road leading to the Nungambakkam tennis stadium.

It was my maiden sports assignment – the Gold Flake Open, in 1998 – a time when the tobacco giants were not banned from sponsoring sporting events. The stands were bursting at the seams. The crowd went from being ecstatic to ballistic, with incessant high-decibel chants of 'Becker, Becker', even before the world's biggest tennis legend gave the spectators *darshan.*

The first match was a classic David-versus-Goliath clash. Expectations of a straight-set victory with a record number of aces and the trademark Becker aggression, were as high as Jack's beanstalk. The 'Boom Boom' German had every soul out there eating out of his big strong palm. A bevy of Page 3 beauties clad in size-zero T-shirts were belting out Silk Smitha style romantic verses! And why not? A tall, well built, handsome, six-time Grand Slam singles champion, an Olympic gold medallist, the youngest winner of the men's singles crown at Wimbledon, was pitted against an unseeded Gerard Solves. And then the action started. And ended. The stunned silence throughout the game was only interrupted by Becker's angry outbursts over some service and line calls 60 minutes later. Even before we could rub our moist eyes in disbelief, the stadium became as quiet as the Indian contingent at Sharjah when Javed Miandad pulled a Chetan Sharma full toss over mid wicket for a last-ball winning six. The greatest of them all had to eat humble pie: the mighty Becker had crashed out, losing 4-6, 6-3, 6-2 to a relatively unknown, unseeded opponent at that.

At press conferences, the front row seats are vantage points to pin down the interviewee. Or so I was told. As a slim, energetic 24-year-old, edging past the veterans to grab a coveted seat was no problem. There I was, sporting an orange-and-black striped shirt, face to face with a world champion I had admired throughout my adolescence. A tired and justifiably exasperated Becker was in no mood to explain his shocking defeat. Hardly

5 seconds after his entry, I fired the first volley. 'Boris, did you throw away the match?' It elicited no answer except a glare, the kind that Stefan Edberg probably got during all those 35 encounters between 1984 and 1996! The IMG officials, particularly Media Manager Craig Gabriel – certainly no Angel Gabriel to a rookie journalist – looked at me as if I had committed blasphemy. The debater in me surfaced, ignoring those disapproving glances, and I shot off my second question. 'Boris, do you believe you played to your full potential?' It pierced through the 6 foot 2 inch-star like a flaming arrow. I could see fire in Becker's eyes as he struggled to mask his outrage with a toned-down admonition: 'If you ask me such questions, I will leave this press conference.' I didn't know there was a Censor Board for press conferences! The tournament officials were livid and looked as if they had gulped down tins of castor oil, as they tried to shout me down, probably in a bid to assuage the frayed nerves of their biggest crowd puller. At the end of the day, experience counts. A senior journalist from Reuters followed up my 'crime' with an almost identical poser but in a manner that the furious champion could hardly threaten to walk out: 'Do you give your opponent full credit for his victory?' Becker paused and then made a feeble attempt to answer it, punctuating his response with innuendoes directed at me, as the hysterical fans who had been laying siege to the conference hall, began to barge into the venue.

The drama after the press conference was more intense! Minutes after the vanquished legend was escorted out of the room, the tournament director, Brian Cooney, a tough-looking

Australian, as tall and well built as Becker himself, walked up to me and with his hands on his hips, and bellowed: 'I hope you are suitably embarrassed. Where did you pick that up from? How could you ever, ever ask the world's greatest tennis player such an idiotic question? I feel like ripping that media pass off your neck. I hope I don't see you tomorrow.'

Honestly, I was taken aback. Taken aback by what I thought was much ado about what was a legitimate question. Taken aback because I had genuinely meant no offence. To a young journalist, the message seemed to be: Diplomacy is the better part of free speech! An improvised maxim that I swore to observe in the breach.

2

AMAZING GRACE

FEW FROM MY GENERATION would have grown up without watching a bearded gentleman on 'The World This Week'. *The Hindu* newspaper, Madhu Trehan's 'News Track' and this show were part of any English teacher's prescription for those who wanted to hone their communication skills and general knowledge. In Don Bosco, the Library period involved a trip to the Audio Visual Hall where a recording of 'The World This Week' and 'News Track' would be screened. After graduating from Loyola college, I vividly recall a close friend and my school and college senior – Nirmal Sanjeevi – telling me to 'write to Prannoy Roy and join his team'. I must confess that it felt quite daunting. Dr. Roy had just started 'The News Tonight' on Doordarshan. It was only after passing out of Law School that I shot off a letter to NDTV in classic prose. In hindsight, it comes across as puerile.

'Nurtured on your inimitable news culture that projects the truth test "seeing is believing", I spread my ware before you in the enclosed CV so you can see and believe that I possess the right mettle for a slot in your band of livewire journalists. If my credentials catch your fancy, do give me a shout.'

All right, not just puerile, but also audacious!

Jennifer Arul, a family friend for decades and the mother of my classmate, David, called to ask me to drop in at her Pantheon Road bungalow with a revised and simple application. That was perhaps the first lesson in television – use simple and short sentences. Farah Sayeed, one of the Chennai correspondents, had put in her papers as she was going to the U.S. to join her husband. I was shortlisted to fill that vacancy. Jennifer was keen to have someone with a legal background, what with the slew of court battles that had to be covered. And of course, the known devil factor!

My interview was fixed for 10 a.m. on 27 of December 1997 at the Taj Connemara. I was to meet the then General Manager of NDTV and one of its co-founders, K.V.L. Narayan Rao, son of Gen. K.V. Krishna Rao, the former Governor of Jammu & Kashmir. I reached the hotel well on time. I wasn't wearing a tie or a suit; I wasn't even clad in what you'd call formal attire: maroon full-sleeved shirt and khaki trousers with a slightly fancy belt! Much later, I came to know that red was almost NDTV's official colour.

I called from the lobby. 'Good Morning, Mr. Rao. I'm Sanjay Pinto. I'd like to meet you.'

'Hi, Sanjay. Please give me 5 minutes.'

I waited for a while and soon the hotel Reception informed me that I could go up to Mr. Rao's suite. I had seen him earlier so, unlike many others, I was not intimidated by his height and build. Mr. Rao 'cut to the chase' (one of his favourite expressions) with a simple poser: 'Sanjay, why television? You've studied law, you've written the Civil Services Exam; is this your last resort?' Despite my years of debating, I was taken aback but regained my composure quickly.

'This is not my last resort. This is my best bet.'

It seemed to have passed muster with Mr. Rao. The interview went on for about 10 minutes.

'Sanjay, we will let you know in a few days. Thank you for coming.'

As I left the suite, several thoughts flashed across my mind. Did I dress appropriately? Did I come across as over-confident? Were my answers to the point? Did he size me up positively? Did I play to my natural strengths?

The New Year came. January passed; mid-February went by. Not a squeak from NDTV. In those days we had no mobile phones. I remember sitting next to the telephone all day, intermittently checking if it was working! On the 16th of February, my phone went dead. The telephone exchange came up with the stock reply: 'Cable fault, Sir.' Murphy's Law in operation. The next day, it sprang back to life with a call. Jennifer Arul was on the line.

'Sanjay, was your phone out of order? The Head Office was trying to reach you. Mr. Rao wants to have a word with you. Can you please call him at 11 a.m.?'

'Yes, Aunty. It was down yesterday. I didn't know it was live until you called. I will call Mr. Rao at 11. Thank you, Aunty.'

'Sanjay, no more Aunty. Just call me 'Jennifer' or 'Jen', ok?'

'Sure, Jen.'

Was that a clue that I had been selected? The next couple of hours seemed like decades.

At 11, with bated breath, I called Mr. Rao's office. His secretary K. Basker answered, and put him on the line.

'Sanjay, are you still very keen about that job?'

I took a deep breath.

'Not very keen, Mr. Rao. I'm hell bent!'

'In that case, you can have it! Welcome to NDTV.''

I was asked to join by the 20th of February. It was right after the serial bomb blasts that had rocked Coimbatore. In a few months, the elections were upon us. And there was no looking back. I had my baptism by fire. As everyone was so caught up with poll fever, the mandatory last round with the Roys was dispensed with in my case, but I was determined to have my *darshan*!

I sought an appointment with Prannoy and Radhika Roy through their trusted lieutenant Hannah Isaac. When I got a confirmation, I applied for leave and travelled to Delhi. I was too much of a rookie at the time to fly, so I took the Tamil Nadu Express. It was an arduous 36-hour journey. Fortunately, I had company. My close friend Albert Rao, who was still preparing for the Civil Services Examination, accompanied me. We stayed at the YMCA Guest House.

When I entered the NDTV Headquarters in Archana Complex, I felt like the character Apple Singh at Lord's from the commercial! From a small bureau in Cison's Complex in Egmore, Chennai, to a sprawling set up in Greater Kailash in Delhi, it was quite a change. It was about 9 a.m. Rajdeep Sardesai was among the few people in the newsroom. The Political Editor of Star News, Rajdeep led by example, chairing morning meetings, not over the telephone. He saw me and shouted; 'Hi Sanjay! Welcome.' Rajdeep assigned a producer, Arjun Hardas, to give me a guided tour of the office. I met many of my colleagues with whom I had only interacted on the phone or email.

It was about 11 a.m. The Roys had their office at the end of the newsroom. The door was ajar. Arjun walked right in with me in tow. Prannoy Roy was standing inside looking at a big plasma screen. Arjun whispered something to him. Prannoy turned to me and with his trademark smile told me something that I still cannot get over. 'Oh Sanjay. Hello. I see you all the time on TV!' For the first time in my life I was speechless. Here was a man I had grown up watching and admiring on TV and this is how he greets a cub reporter of his channel? The warmth he exuded is worth a separate chapter. I had a more formal sit down meeting with Dr. Roy and Mrs. Roy in a few minutes. 'We value your energy,' was what Mrs. Roy said, patting me on my back, as I left their office.

I also remember disagreeing with him on a group email over what was viewed as a commercial plug for a windshield manufacturer. I stuck to my guns. After a lot of back and forth, Dr. Roy replied: 'Ok. If you're convinced, I am. Full faith.' How often can one argue with the owner of the channel and have him publicly accept your point of view? That's how genuine the Roys truly are.

Fourteen years later.

I had decided to move on and plunge into legal practice.

This is what Prannoy texted me on 13 September 2012, at 5:20 p.m., minutes before I was to cut a farewell cake in the bureau.

'Dear Sanjay, I am so sad to get your message. Especially sad for Radhika and me. We shall treat this as our child discovering himself and going off on a break – to return soon one day. Follow your dreams. It's the only way to live. God bless you Sanjay. Lots of love from Radhika and me to your wonderful wife and babies.'

The Roys were never bosses. Only role models. What amazing grace.

3

A MOUTHFUL OF NEWS!

JUDGMENTS PRONOUNCED IN COURT are not complicated or boring. Not when you have legal training. Court proceedings never befuddled me; they were stimulating. If anything, my stories from the court halls only renewed my belief that 'the grass is greener on the other side'.

There are and can be no watertight compartmentalised beats in television. A TV journalist has to be adept in legalese as well as in the language of Science & Technology. But while many of my counterparts would prefer a rocket launch at Sriharikota to a court judgment, my choice was a no brainer! Jennifer Arul, or 'Jen' as she preferred to be called, who once described herself as 'half mother, half boss' in NDTV, (she had known me from the time I was half the height of her dining table, as her son David's classmate) too didn't quite fancy court hearings. So as the 'lawyer in the office' almost all court assignments were mine. That was well before I had heard of the McDonald's tag line 'I'm loving it'!

Tamil Nadu was home to some of the most intense electoral battles, not just at the hustings but in court rooms too. The AIADMK Chief J. Jayalalithaa was faced with a slew of corruption cases slapped on her by her arch-rival, the DMK patriarch M. Karunanidhi. The AIADMK legal think tank had viewed the TANSI case as the biggest thorn in their side. Jayalalithaa had been accused of buying Government property when she was the Chief Minister. The trial court had convicted her in this land deal, as well as in the Pleasant Stay Hotel case involving the alleged violation of building norms. This meant disqualification from contesting elections. Although Jayalalithaa could not contest the 2001 assembly poll, she was sworn in as Chief Minister by Governor Fathima Beevi. This controversial decision that was struck down by the Supreme Court a few months later, resulting in Jayalalithaa stepping down and anointing her chosen one – a relatively unknown O. Paneerselvam – to keep the Chief Minister's chair warm.

The journey from Poes Garden to Fort St. George now hinged on an appeal in a higher tier of judicial wisdom. The verdict in a packed court room on a December morning would determine her political future.

I had sent a backgrounder on the cases to the office, which was aired on 'Breakfast News'.

As I was scribbling a few notes on a chit for my live reports through the day, Sreenivasan Jain, my senior colleague in Delhi, called.

'Sanj, all set? What's it looking like?'

'Hi Vasu. It may be an acquittal in the TANSI case. Not sure about Pleasant Stay.'

'What are you saying?'

'Vasu, two months ago, the judge had questioned the Special Public Prosecutor if there was proof that the signature on the TANSI sale deed was indeed that of Jayalalithaa. If that plank of the prosecution is hit, in my opinion, the case will not stand.'

Vasu had a keen interest in court battles. I always had the feeling that his elder brother Gopal Jain, a Supreme Court lawyer, used to feed him with relevant nuggets of information from the corridors of courts.

'Alright, tiger. Will hear you on air when it comes out.'

The pindrop silence ensured that one even heard the loud 'Shhhh' that heralded the arrival of Justice N. Dhinakar (not to be confused with Justice P.D. Dinakaran).

A mobile phone started beeping; it kept getting louder with each beep! Usually, the phone would be confiscated and the owner hauled up for contempt and fined. But with so many people inside such a packed hall, each almost doing a Nataraja pose, pinning down the culprit from whose pocket the decibels emanated, was just not possible. Only I knew!

A few intelligence officials were standing next to me. It was not a coincidence. I heard that the last time when they called their bosses with inputs, they were given a dressing down. 'Why are you giving us stale information? We already heard it on NDTV!' Flashing news first was something that gave me a high! So the sleuths made it a point to look over my shoulders, rather into my phone, like ill-prepared students in an exam hall. For sensational verdicts, I would often type out two text messages on the mobile and save them in my drafts folder. For instance, 'Madras High Court grants bail to xxx' or 'Madras High Court rejects the bail plea of xxx.' Given my legal background, sniffing out the verdict even as the judge was reading it out was not too difficult.

If cases crawl in courts, time sometimes flies when the operative part of judgments are read out. My pre-typed messages were sent in a jiffy. Justice Dhinakar had allowed both the appeals, acquitting Jayalalithaa in both the TANSI transaction and the Pleasant Stay Hotel case. *'Tansi property was neither a trust property, nor was it under the control of the government. Therefore, there's no question of Ms Jayalalitha purchasing government property. The Code of Conduct doesn't apply.'* In the Pleasant Stay case, the judge held that the prosecution had failed to establish 'mens rea' (criminal intention) in the process.

Getting out of the court hall was a struggle as I had perched myself quite close to the Bench to be able to hear the pronouncement. Almost everyone in the crowd was in a tearing hurry to inform someone or the other about the development. This was the pre-OB-van period where breaking news had to be through phone-ins. There were two missed calls on my mobile in the space of a minute, following my text message, that I couldn't hear inside the court hall, as my phone was silent. I picked up the third call and was connected to the PCR (Production Control Room) as I made a dash downstairs to get sound bites from Jayalalithaa's ecstatic lawyers. Vishnu Som was the anchor in the Delhi studio. My phone signal was not very clear. This was before the 'What an Idea, Sirji' period! I began to rattle off facts of the case. Suddenly in the middle of my live report, I stopped speaking. Vishnu thought he had lost the audio link. It took about 10 seconds for me to recover and resume my phone-in. A jubilant party worker who was distributing *ladoo*s had stuffed one into my mouth! I have never gobbled a sweet that fast in my life! Perhaps this was a reward for not just reporting the news first but getting it right too, proving that 'breaking news' and accuracy can go together!

4

PM'S CORDON

YOUNG BLOOD OFTEN PUSHES you to do things that in hindsight you would never dare to. Your first job is that stage of your life when all you want to do is prove yourself. Now; actually yesterday! Covering the Prime Minister would give any 24-year-old a high. The BJP-led National Democratic Alliance was in power at the Centre and Atal Bihari Vajpayee was the captain of a ship that faced icebergs from allies! Not just subtle pulls and pressures, that any coalition suffers from, but loud and visible manifestations of discord.

The PM was to arrive by a special flight in the morning. The press corps was at the airport a good hour in advance. The State Information Department and the Press Information Bureau (PIB) had issued passes for coverage of his arrival and departure at the airport. For some reason, the Special Protection Group (SPG) decided to ban mobile phones inside the enclosure meant for the media, overlooking the tarmac.

For a 24-hour news channel, not breaking the news on what the PM says is a crime.

'Why can't we take our phones inside? It defeats the purpose of our presence here!' I tried to argue with the officers.

'Sorry. For security reasons we can't allow it.'

'But will you agree to do your duty if you were asked to deposit your service revolver outside?'

The officer was taken aback and went to consult his superior. He returned in two minutes.

'All right, you can take your phones but only after we check each instrument.'

'Sure. Thanks. Please frisk us and all that we are carrying thoroughly.'

The AIADMK was an integral part of the NDA. But the party was peeved by the Centre's handling of the Cauvery tangle and had decided to stay away from the airport to receive the PM. The symbolism was not lost on us.

The PM landed and was received by the ruling DMK top brass and senior bureaucrats. As Mr. Vajpayee finished accepting all the bouquets and shawls, he moved towards his convoy. The good lord knows what came over me. I darted across holding my mike that was connected to the camera, almost dragging cameraperson Srini along. The black cats surrounding the VVIP glared at me as I landed right in front of Atalji. For a moment, I was dumbstruck. This was the PM after all.

'What do you want me to say? I am happy to be in Chennai.'

'Sir, are you happy to be in Chennai without your alliance party leader here to receive you?'

'I am happy to be in Chennai. Thank you.'

A rookie journalist clearly doesn't get the better of a veteran political leader. But this was just round one!

As the convoy left, I was encircled by the entire media crowd and found myself addressing a sort of parallel press conference!

'What did he say?'

'Oh, nothing except that he is happy to be in Chennai!'

'That's it?'

'Yes, you saw me, right'.

It was just a ten second interface and a potentially dangerous one at that. Cameraperson Srini was furious. 'Do you know the commandos could have shot us? Why did you run like that?'

'I'm sorry. But nothing happened. Do I look like a security threat?' My inexperience was all too obvious!

'PM's Press Meet at Raj Bhavan in half an hour,' a PIB official screamed rather hysterically.

The drive to the Raj Bhavan from the airport during peak hour traffic seemed endless. Vehicles were moving at a snail's pace, bumper to bumper over the Guindy bridge. The saving grace was that the entire media contingent was stuck in traffic, except of course, those who hadn't come to the airport and were on their way directly to the Raj Bhavan from their homes or offices.

Reaching the venue a few minutes before a PM's press meet was not without excitement. For a change, I couldn't grab a seat in the front row.

The PM walked in. A press statement was distributed and cordless mikes were passed around. I managed to get my hand on one and stood up to ask my question. But the Doordarshan Correspondent was given the honour of asking the first question. From what I vaguely remember, it was hardly newsworthy.

My turn came next. Again, I was prevented from quizzing the PM by a few grey eminences who insisted that a senior journalist be given the opportunity ahead of the others.

I got my chance at the third attempt. 'Mr. Prime Minister, in your statement you have hailed the constitution of the Cauvery River Authority as a landmark achievement of your Govt. But your most important ally, Ms. Jayalalithaa, has called it a fraud perpetrated on the people of Tamil Nadu. How do you explain this, sir?' I had travelled to the delta districts of Tiruvarur and Thanjavur for a ground zero report on the plight of farmers dependent on the Cauvery water.

I looked suitably pleased with myself, like the *sardar* at a shareholders meet in that India Bulls TV commercial!

Mr. Vajpayee didn't seem annoyed but he took some time to answer that, reassuring the people of Tamil Nadu that justice would be done.

There were supplementary questions from others, based on mine, indicating that I had contributed to a news angle!

At the end of the interaction, an official came to offer unsolicited advice. 'Young man, please don't do that again.'

I still don't know if he meant the tenor of the question or my security cordon bit, or the mobile phone wrangling. Any which way, I got noticed!

5

SUNDAY PASSAGE

NO NEW RECRUIT IN a 24-hour television news channel bureau can afford to switch off on a Sunday. 'Work is worship' is the best rejoinder to 'Thou Shall Keep the Sabbath Holy'. For more than two years, I underwent baptism by fire. This meant, among other things, working on Sundays.

It was the last Sunday before Christmas. Just before communion hymn, my mobile phone vibrated. I initially thought it was an overzealous Input Editor wanting to know more about my day plan or about some PTI report. As it just didn't seem to stop, I genuflected and left the mass midway at St.Theresa's Church.

It was the ever-efficient and affable Hannah Isaac, the Manager at the office of Dr. Prannoy Roy and Mrs. Radhika Roy, on the line.

'Hi Sanjay. Sorry to bother you. This is an emergency. Maya Mirchandani survived a bomb blast in Colombo. She is on her way back to Delhi via Chennai. The Roys would like you to be with her at the airport when she arrives and help in any way you can.'

'Oh sure. That's my duty. What time is she landing?'

'Let me send you her flight details.'

Maya Mirchandani used to cover the external affairs beat and was on an assignment in Colombo tracking the election campaign of President Chandrika Kumaratunga. A suicide bomber managed to scale a fence and, as the Lankan leader stopped to answer a question from Maya a few metres away from the car, there was an explosion. Maya fell down but miraculously survived the blast; as did President Kumaratunga, who escaped with an eye injury. Thirty-six people, including the President's driver, bodyguards, and a Deputy Inspector General of Police were killed. Maya's cameraperson Gaurav Bakshi was quite the real hero; he had kept the camera on and recorded the blast!

My headquarters was concerned about the trauma our crew would have been subjected to, and wanted to make their passage back home, via Chennai, hassle free.

I called an IPS Officer friend, Karuna Sagar, to put me on to a contact at the Airport.

'Karuna, I just need some facilitation for my colleagues at the International Terminal. They have just been through a blast and are traumatized. Don't want them to go through any needless procedures here.'

'No problem. I will speak to Surya Prasad and give you his number. Call him in five minutes.'

M.V.N. Surya Prasad was the Deputy Commissioner of Police, Airport Security, whom I had briefly met at a party about a week ago.

'Hi boss. I'm Sanjay Pinto…Karuna…'

'Hi Sanjay. Sagar told me everything. Don't worry. When you reach the airport, please call me. I will send an officer to take you inside so you can receive your friends at the immigration counter.'

'Thank you boss. That's sweet of you.'

I reached the airport at about 3 o'clock. The flight was slightly delayed.

Meanwhile, there was a call from my head office.

'Maya has footage of the blast. It's priceless footage. It's not on a beta tape. It's in a different format. You have to collect the tape from her and have it uplinked to us asap.'

By this time, word had spread that an NDTV crew had survived the blast and were on their way back through Chennai. A few local TV channel reporters landed up in the hope of getting a firsthand account from Maya!

I called my office to check if that was alright.

'Please avoid that if you can. They must be tired, so let's not subject them to a mini press conference at this juncture. And we need to air our precious footage first with Maya's account in the studio for the 9 o'clock news.'

I informed the crews that Maya wouldn't be available for comment but one of them shot back: 'If it had not been your colleague, let's say if it were a politician returning after surviving a blast, wouldn't you also be here trying to get a sound bite?'

'Yes, of course,' I retorted. 'Just that in this case, she is not just a survivor but an eyewitness as well. And we have the first right of airing. I myself am not getting her on camera here. My office had decided to give her some time and she will talk about this after she returns to Delhi. I will give you a heads up and if my channel decides to permit others to cut live with a credit band, you could use that.'

They saw my point but refused to budge. To be fair, in their shoes, I too would have waited to give it a shot.

I bought a bunch of flowers and two tetra packs of orange juice for Maya and Gaurav. Surya Prasad passed on the number of an officer who was waiting for me at the entrance of the terminal. We identified each other. The young sub inspector escorted me inside after the mandatory security check and frisking. I waited for the flight to land.

Maya and Gaurav were among the first few passengers to emerge and were visibly relieved to see me at the immigration point. They both gave me a warm hug.

Maya looked dazed. 'Sanjay, still can't believe we are alive! Thank you for coming here. Oh God, we were soaked in blood and it took us more than an hour to wash ourselves.'

'Thank God you are safe. Your connecting flight to Delhi leaves in an hour. Our media friends are waiting outside to interview you.'

'No Sanjay, No. I'm in no state to talk about it.'

'I know. I understand, Maya. But you know how we in the media will try, anyway! It's their right to try.'

'Yes, of course but what to do.'

'We need to "smuggle" both of you to the domestic terminal!'

But how! There was no link between the two buildings and passengers had to come out of one terminal to get into the other. It was about 300 metres between the two points.

I called our driver Devaraj. Our car had an NDTV sticker and tinted glasses.

'Devaraj, slowly move the car to the domestic entrance now and then suddenly open and close the doors, honk a few times and pretend to leave in a tearing hurry.'

It's a standard tactic politicians use to give the media the slip! It worked for us this time!

The TV crews first looked at the car advancing towards the domestic side. But their eyes were fixed at the international terminal entrance. But, they heared the staged sudden activity, and thought that Maya had got into our car and the whole lot ran behind as it left.

I used the opportunity to sneak Maya and Gaurav into the domestic airport. I had no choice. Gaurav gave me the tape and I left in a taxi as my car had left with a few camera crews in tow!

Now came the next big challenge. Transferring the footage into the Beta format. This was a world exclusive. And it had to be uplinked to Delhi in about an hour. Our cosy little Chennai Bureau in Cisons Complex didn't have the facility to transfer footage from one format to the other.

In a sort of eureka moment, I called a friend in Ennadu Television for help.

'Come in ten minutes as the Editors will leave in a short while.'

The ETV office was in Parsn Complex. I made a dash for it. It took about half an hour for the transfer. The footage was shocking. There was clearly divine protection for our team. My admiration for the cameraperson Gaurav shot up like Jack's beanstalk. The blast was so deafening that the 'nat' sounds had to be dipped on the edit machine.

It was another mad rush back to our bureau office to uplink the footage.

As the engineer in the MCR – Master Control Room – in Delhi told our video editor Ravi Varma, 'feed is fine', I almost sank in my chair.

I called Delhi to say that the footage was sent.

Then came a different bombshell. 'Ok Sanjay, what story are you filing today?'

I felt like reciting the 'Our Father In Heaven…' that I had stopped midway during the morning mass!

6

DRAVID-IAN TWIST!

A SPAT THAT TURNS into a wonderful rapport constitutes a typical Kollywood storyline. Strangely, this also has characterised my interaction with many newsmakers I have covered. Barring, of course, some outstanding exceptions! An initial crack led to cementing of ties with the 'Wall' of Indian cricket.

In March 2001, the Indian team manager had imposed a gag order on players during the Border-Gavaskar trophy series. It was a BCCI decision to have just one pre-match briefing by the captain so that the cricketers could focus on their game and nothing else. The fear was that comments by other players could be misread or quoted out of context or twisted to look like digs at others in the dressing room, or opinions blurted out may come across as critical of the skipper's calls, all of which would put unnecessary pressure on the team and individuals.

Other than net practice, the only activity permitted was a social outreach programme. It was not just big corporates that banked on the popularity of cricketers; quite a few NGOs had roped in players to champion their cause. Every break between matches in a series would often be punctuated with visits to an orphanage or an appearance up at sponsored concerts or mere interaction with special children.

After the day's practice I used to stake out at the Taj Coromandel where the team was put up, hoping to get that extra interview. The players had just finished participating in a celebrity dinner in aid of an orphanage. A few TV crews were allowed to get sound bites from the players but only on the event. 'Not a word on the game.' That was how strict the brief was. I approached Rahul Dravid for his take. Honestly, I didn't need the BCCI to lead me to temptation, I found the way myself!

'Rahul, this evening was a gentleman's game as well, right? How will your interaction with these children help you in your innings tomorrow?'

A smart-alec stunt didn't pass muster with the no-nonsense cricketer. Rahul pushed the mike down and reprimanded me: 'I knew you would do this.' As he walked away, I realised I had made a mistake. I shouldn't have even tried that trick. But at that age and stage in your career, you do goof up sometimes.

I went up to him the next morning as he got off the bus. 'Rahul, I'm sorry about last evening. I was just trying to get a spin on a story but I genuinely didn't mean to force the pace in that manner. I hope we can put that behind us.'

Rahul put his kit down for a minute and looked at me with his trademark boyish smile. 'Hey, don't think too much about it.

I'm cool. But you know we are not authorized to speak on the matches. That's why I had to cut you short. But nice try, man!'

My respect for Rahul went up since that morning. A champion of his stature could have easily boycotted a rookie reporter but he chose to be gracious and let it be. But it's not as if I would give up!

Nineteen months later, in October 2002, Rahul was on the verge of equalling a record set by Sir Everton Weekes: five Test centuries in consecutive innings. After three hundreds on the trot in England, the stylish batsman retired hurt owing to a painful bout of cramps but not before notching up exactly a century against the West Indies. The second Test against the Caribbean team was in Chennai. This was the pre-sponsored-interview period. Most TV channels didn't even have fully fledged sports desks. I was lucky that I got to cover all the cricket action in Chennai because my boss and the only other correspondent in the bureau, Jennifer Arul, hated the game, with her antipathy had only been reinforced after a senior player had, in 1996, demanded two lakh rupees for an interview!) You got exclusive interviews with cricketers on the strength of your knowledge of the game, your rapport with the players, and persistence. Having made up with Rahul, I had no hesitation in asking for an interview. My only worry was whether he would allow himself to be distracted by a television interaction just before his possible tryst with history.

I pitched it to him in the most straightforward fashion.

'Rahul, I know you must be concentrating on reaching that milestone. Millions of your fans must be more nervous than you are! How about an interview to tell them what's going through your mind? I'll take only five minutes.'

'Ah. Not sure if I want to talk about it. But...' Rahul took about a minute to think; 'Alright. Shall we do it after the nets? Short interview. For old time's sake!'

'Wow, that's great. Thanks a ton. Should I set it up opposite the dressing room?'

'Either there or at the Cricket Club. Actually, you decide where it will look better.'

'At the stands outside the dressing room is fine!'

The interview went on for fourteen minutes. Rahul was relaxed and denied reports that he was under pressure. 'I play for the team not for records. If it happens, fine. I'm not going to be too conscious about it.'

That evening, a friend Vasanth Raghuvir, managing trustee of the Shakti Foundation had organised a dinner for special children at the Taj by the poolside, to which she invited the entire Indian team, through her NGO's brand ambassador Anil Kumble. Vasanth knew that I covered cricket extensively and loved making speeches.

'Sanjay, why don't you welcome the gathering?'

I accepted the offer at once.

The entire cricket team turned up.

I made a very short speech. 'If Mohammed cannot come to the mountain, the mountain will come to Mohammed. In much the same way, our cricketing heroes have all come this evening to show how much they care for the differently-abled. Tomorrow is a special day for one of our players. May I also request all of you to please say a little prayer for Rahul to equal Sir Everton Weekes' record.'

After the function, Rahul came up to me to say that he was touched by what I did. I could sense that he too was beginning to respect me. It felt good. Especially against the backdrop of my initial brush with him.

Rahul didn't go on to reach that goal. But like he said, he wasn't after records.

My interaction with him only got warmer with time. In 2004, at the Asia Cup in Colombo and Dambulla, I was assigned six sponsored interviews with Rahul. For every single interview, he arrived on the dot. Once, he texted that he may be late by 5 minutes, but ended up on time. Such was the professionalism of the man. On the day of the last interview, Rahul introduced me to his wife Vijetha in the lobby of the Taj Samudra. 'Sanjay's one guy who respects our time and who once said sorry and truly was.' I choked. That was the best certificate I ever got, that too from a champion who could have easily pushed me to the wall!

7

IN THE FIRING LINE

I REMEMBER THE SHOCK on the face of chocolate hero 'Maddy' (actor Madhavan) during an exclusive interview at his aero-modelling venue near Red Hills when I told him how I used to wait every Thursday at 8:30 p.m. for a serial on Doordarshan, titled 'Sea Hawks'. Maddy had played the role of a young Coast Guard officer Preeth, with Niki Aneja, among others. Despite being the son of a business tycoon, Preeth took to the white uniform that paid him just six thousand rupees a month.

'Sanjay, you still remember all those minute details!"

'Yes, I do, Maddy. That and several other serials like "Udan", "Rajni", not to forget Shah Rukh Khan's "Fauji"! Many of them were so inspiring that it's hard to forget even some of the dialogues. Remember the "I say chaps" line in Fauji?'

'*Baap re*! You journos never forget eh!'

'Nothing to do with journos!'

So when an assignment on coastal patrolling came up, I grabbed it with both my hands. And feet! The fear of sea-sickness was at the back of my mind but I let it remain just there – at the back of my mind!

Cases of smuggling of narcotic substances and even arms and ammunition from Sri Lanka to Tamil Nadu through the Dhanushkodi coast were widely reported. How exactly was the coast being patrolled? The danger innocent Tamil fishermen are exposed to as they cast their nets: that was the storyline. My bid to get on a Coast Guard vessel seemed mired in procedures and a lot of avoidable protocol! But the Naval Detachment in Rameshwaram didn't make a fuss. Commander Francis and a young Navy officer were on duty. They received us as if we were childhood buddies, and were ready to take us on board.

Dhanushkodi was called a 'ghost town' because a cyclone had ravaged the place decades ago. A dilapidated memorial for those who died stood testimony on the blazing hot sand.

It was almost 12 noon. The sun was blazing fiercely down on us. I had forgotten to bring a cap.

'Here take mine' said an ever-so-friendly Commander Francis, as he placed a smart military fatigue cap on my head.

There was a small naval patrol motor boat on the shore. It was like a catamaran, about seven feet long and four feet wide making it a tight squeeze for the four of us; the two navy officers, my cameraperson, and myself. The height of the boat was approximately two feet. There was a small motor at the back and oars at the side.

'Do you know swimming?'

'I don't commander. I'm a YMCA first day swimming course drop out because the water was too cold! But my cameraperson can splash around a bit.'

'This water is hot but never mind; I'll save you if we topple! The sea is a bit choppy today.'

The defence tribe have a way of speaking that can give you the jitters. But there was no turning back!

'We'll go upto the fifth island, that's the IBL – the international boundary line – between India and Sri Lanka. This boat doesn't go too fast so we will make it in a couple of hours. Hold on tight to the side.'

'Will the waves come in?'

'They will. They won't harm you! Just remove your wallet and your mobile phone from that clip on your belt and keep them inside your shirt. Here, put them into this plastic cover.'

'Thank you, commander. You're giving me a whole kit!'

Under normal circumstances, I would have thrown up at least a few times. But when you are tense and have bigger things on your mind, or in your heart, or your heart in your mouth, routine functions take a back seat!

The cap was a saviour. I felt like a Casabianca on the burning deck and would have easily fainted without it!

A couple of times, our boat ran out of diesel. The young officer who was steering us, went behind to fill the tank from a large can on the boat.

As he covered the diesel can, he pulled out a casserole from under a thick rubber sheet.

'Lemon rice and prawn curry. Please help yourself.'

'Oh thanks. But I'll avoid eating anything now. I may throw up!'

Commander Francis suddenly looked a bit concerned. It wasn't about my delayed lunch but something more serious.

A large ship could be seen in the distance. It was moving towards us. Commander Francis had a good hard look through his binoculars.

Reaching for the walkie-talkie, he shouted: 'This is Indian Navy Patrol, come in…'

There was no response.

Commander Francis copied the instruction, this time with another line: 'We have a Star News TV crew on board.'

'Commander, is there something wrong?'

'No, don't worry.'

That sounded like his earlier 'I'll save you if we topple' assurance!

'Sir, what's the problem? Please tell us.'

'Sanjay, that looks like a Sri Lankan navy vessel. Those chaps can just open fire if they suspect that this is an LTTE suicide boat. They don't take chances and sometimes don't bother to check.'

The instructions were repeated but there was still no response.

I said a little prayer. There was nothing else I could do. I instinctively pulled out my mobile phone. It obviously had no signal. This was the pre-roaming period. And in any case, we were on the high seas.

Our two member navy team decided to move closer to the approaching vessel.

'Put up your hands,' Commander Francis instructed all of us.

Like obedient soldiers we followed the command.

This was to denote a surrender and prevent a reckless reaction from the other side.

'This is the fifth island. This is the International Boundary Line. From the sixth island onwards is Sri Lankan territorial water.'

I nodded but kept silent. This is the ride of my life, I thought.

Mercifully, there was no firing so far. For the next few minutes, all I could hear was the sound of the waves hitting our little boat. All I could sense was my heart pounding. The climax was yet to come.

In half an hour it did. As we inched closer, we spotted a flag on the vessel and the words 'Indian Coast Guard' painted on it! This was the vessel we had initially intended to jump on to. Ironically, it turned into an object of apprehension and fear. My cameraperson began focussing.

The officer on board looked miffed.

'What are you doing here? No. No. Don't shoot.'

That was our prayer all along, I chuckled.

'Please put the camera down.'

Commander Francis and the Coast Guard officer had a chat and we turned back.

I was tempted to take up the lemon rice and prawn curry offer. But I decided not to risk tainting my 'no throwing up' record. Instead, I stood up to do a piece to camera from the border.

'Should we claim daily allowance for international travel as we were at the international boundary line?' I joked with my suitably relieved colleague. Perhaps the navy bravado had rubbed off on me slightly!

8

NELLORE IDLIS

IN A TELEVISION NEWS BUREAU with just two Correspondents, off-days are never set in stone. That was among the first set of instructions handed over to me when I joined NDTV. Our fair 5-day-week roster ensured that we got one day off on the weekend and one weekday. The more pious Jennifer Arul opted for Sundays and Mondays and I chose Fridays and Saturdays. In the late nineties, NDTV used to more than pamper its employees. A shoot before 8 a.m. meant breakfast on the house; between 12 and 3 p.m. earned you lunch; high tea was the norm regardless of shoot timings; and dinner was assured if you worked after 9 p.m. Sundays invariably resulted in a Biriyani feast from Hotel Thayif, which could be smelt from our cosy little Cisons Complex studio (before we moved to the plush C.I.T. Colony office), or from Hotel Ponnuswamy.

No such gastronomical luck was with us on Sunday, 24 January 1999. A popular BJP leader from Nellore, Challa

Ramakrishna Reddy had been hacked to death in front of his home by assailants posing as push-cart vegetable vendors. The distance between Chennai and Nellore was just 175 kilometres, a three-hour drive, as opposed to the 450-odd kilometres from Hyderabad, which was almost eight to nine hours by road. The buck thus stopped at my table. Tension had spread across Andhra Pradesh, resulting in a *bandh* being called in Nellore. The only saving grace was that our Camera Assistant – those days we had them – Srinivasa Rao, alias Sudhir, was Telugu-speaking. Not to mention the smattering of Telugu I had picked up in Loyola College where I was conscripted to this second language (beginners level), as the Hindi which I had chosen was like Greek and Latin to me!

*Bandh*s are not always total. There would be the odd bunk shop selling bananas or at least a tea shop with its shutters only half-down, like the TASMAC liquor outlet in Tamil Nadu. Strangely, there was absolutely nothing open. Nellore resembled a ghost town. The murdered leader was quite a party heavyweight and his supporters went on the rampage. As the needle of suspicion pointed to sympathisers of a rival political party, the CPI(M), a heavy police presence was visible right across town. But we were starving; the only bites we could get were sound bites from political leaders. The only thing fully charged was our camera battery. All hotels and lodges were shut, so there was no question of even discreetly checking in and ordering room service.

The CPI(M) headquarters had a thick security blanket thrown around it. The Chief inside, Jakka Venkaiah, was known to be a stormy petrel. As his unit was being accused by the BJP of being behind the killing, I was advised to tread cautiously with him. 'No provocative questions, or he will flare up,' I was forewarned by local journalists. Frankly, I didn't mind the prospect of growling. I was already hearing enough from my stomach! But Jakka Venkaiah turned out to be very courteous and even complimented me on my effort to pose a question in Telugu!

Our next interview was with Union Minister of State for Home Ch. Vidyasagar Rao, who was camping in Nellore. Tall, fair, and handsome, he could easily pass for a Telugu Film Hero. After a relaxed tête-à-tête, as we were packing up, he thoughtfully turned to me; 'Please stay for a late breakfast.'

The NDTV pride and policy forced me to blurt out. 'That's very kind of you to offer, Sir. Thank you but we have to leave to complete our shooting.'

'When will you eat?'

'After we finish the story, Sir.'

'Rather, where will you eat? Everything is shut.'

I had known of a party spokesperson in Chennai who used to hurriedly draw the curtains in his living room so that we would not get a glimpse of even his dining table, much less offer us even a glass of water! This was a different level of hospitality, that too at a time when his party was in shock and mourning.

Vidyasagar Rao almost forced us to eat *idli*s and *sambar*. I wolfed them down and thanked him profusely while leaving.

That was also a lesson. Since that shoot, I never travelled out of town without dry fruits and biscuits in my bag. Journalists do need to be tough cookies!

9

CHO BE IT!

I HAVE ALWAYS ADMIRED Cho Ramaswamy, much before his *Tuglaq* avatar. His sparkling wit and sarcasm came through even in his film dialogues. But this admiration was initially like any other fan of his. In the summer of 1998 when I joined NDTV (Star News), the election season saw a steady stream of not just top political leaders, but also veteran journalists and commentators marching into our Chennai studio. I was well connected with bureaucrats and journalists from my school and college years, but politicians and actors-turned-observers were a different kettle of fish. The Guest Desk in the Delhi Headquarters informed the bureau that Cho Ramaswamy had been lined up for a discussion with our Political Editor, Rajdeep Sardesai, in the Delhi studio.

Jennifer Arul was in the edit suite putting together a story. If I remember correctly, Ahila Samuel who used to deal with guests and still does, thanks to a well-deserved extension, was out on some work. Cho Ramaswamy walked in wearing a crisp safari suit. I greeted him and introduced myself. He came across as very down-to-earth, almost affable. The peon offered him coffee but he politely refused. Clearing his throat, something that I later realised was like a punctuation mark in his conversations, he turned to me and, in a matter-of-fact tone, said:

'Get me some lipstick.'

I was taken aback and smiled, thinking that he was probably pulling my leg.

'Sorry, Sir?'

'Lipstick, lipstick.'

I sensed that he actually meant it but couldn't fathom why. And for whom?! These were very early days in my career. I went into the edit suite and informed Jennifer about this peculiar request.

'Jen, Cho is asking for lipstick.'

Without batting an eyelid she responded: 'Oh, just open my bag. There's a new Revlon. Give it to him.'

I was still clueless; but did as instructed.

As soon as I handed over the lipstick to Cho, he applied it generously before adjusting the lapel mike and clearing his throat again. I don't think he detected any unease or amusement on my face or perhaps he just didn't care.

After he left, I went up to Jennifer and with justifiable bewilderment and my eyes almost popping out, asked her:

'Jen, what was that?!'

'Forgot to tell you. It's just that he smokes a pipe and his lips have become dark. For the camera, these are normal things people do.'

I must confess that it took a while for the explanation to sink in.

My learning curve had different dimensions. As I interacted more often with Cho, I found him to be extremely sharp and intelligent, the kind of political mentor anyone would be gifted to have; my senior colleague G. C. Shekhar, then with the *Hindustan Times*, still swears by Cho's political perspective.

I will never forget how he once rebutted a BJP spokesperson on a prime time debate who sought to play down alliance pulls and pressures. Party emissaries used to air dash to Chennai at frequent intervals to placate AIADMK Chief Ms. Jayalalithaa, who didn't allow the saffron party to take her support for the National Democratic Alliance, for granted. In his almost brusque style, Cho thundered: 'So Pramod Mahajan and George Fernandes keep coming to Chennai to visit Mahabalipuram?'

While I used to question my Head Office for roping in 'usual suspects' for panel discussions, Cho was one panellist I would readily agree to rustle up for any programme. The pre-discussion chat as the camera, lights, and mike would be set up was something I always longed for. The man's tongue-in-cheek repartee used to remind me of the wit of P. G. Wodehouse, Mark Twain, G.B. Shaw, and Oscar Wilde!

The packed auditorium at his annual lecture at the *Tuglaq* anniversary celebration bore testimony to his popularity and just how the audience lapped up political satire and unbuttoned no-holds-barred analysis. Watching the telecast on a regional TV channel was a treat, better than Chennai Super Kings chasing 250 plus!

The last time I met Cho at his Mandaveli office was sometime in 2009 when I requested him to recommend my membership to the Mylapore Club. With a flourish he pulled out his pen and signed my membership form; quite like the flourish with which he took that lipstick from me the first time we met!

10

SHACKLING THE TRUTH?

LESSONS AFTER A TRAGEDY; that is something we in India almost instinctively try hard to not learn. Not just the government, private bodies and individuals too sail in the same boat; and make others sink. Imagine 28 mentally challenged patients, not being able to escape from a fire that engulfed their shelter turned death trap because they were chained to logs. The incident from Erwadi in Tamil Nadu's Ramanathapuram district, made international headlines. And then there were camera-induced tears and wake-up calls and raids and pious platitudes and enquiry commissions.

Not to forget the first anniversary fanfare, in the run-up to which the government publicity machinery worked overtime. There would be an overkill of press releases and statements, press conferences and both planted and embedded stories; all designed to convince the masses of a healing touch that never was.

Arnab Goswami (most successful television journalists were pretty much born and brought up in NDTV!) had just been promoted as News Editor. Arnab's brief was to drive bureaus to come up with exclusive stories that could be played up. This was when NDTV was producing Star News. I was quite the willing horse in the Chennai bureau.

'Give me something that others don't have, my friend; a cracker of a story that we can go to town with.' Arnab was not the sort who would make the odd call and give you a long rope to deliver. I must admit the man had the persistence of King Bruce's spider!

'Working on some leads, Dada' – a term of endearment many of us used for Arnab – 'Give me a week.'

'You have time till the day before yesterday! Come on, Sanjay, don't tell me that with all your contacts in Tamil Nadu, you can't give me a scoop in a day or two?'

Flattery works well in the media. Even with street smart journalists.

When politicians start making a beeline to accident sites and newspapers bring out special features on an issue, you know that an anniversary of some tragedy is round the corner.

August, 2002: With a surfeit of stories on the reconstruction and reformation in Erwadi splashed all over the media, I decided to do a reality check. Cameraperson Sukumar had just been transferred from Delhi to Chennai and was known to be a seasoned player. This was my first shoot with him.

'Suku, let's do a recce first.' This meant going in without our equipment, as regular visitors.

To enter a shelter for mentally challenged people, we had to remove our shoes and socks and walk on the hot sand. As a little boy, I had relished playing cricket on hot tar roads barefoot and here I was struggling to traverse just a few hundred metres without worrying about getting blisters on my soles.

Arnab must have been praying hard for a big story. When we neared the place, Suku and I looked at each other in horror and disbelief. Despite all the positive news reports, hardly a stone's throw from the site of last year's tragedy, mentally challenged patients were still being chained in this place. I spotted four people: one was chained to a window grill, one to a tree, one to a hook cemented to the floor and one had chains on her ankle but was moving around.

The Supreme Court had taken *suo motu* notice of newspaper reports on chaining of inmates and issued a clear ban on this inhuman practice. The challenge now was to capture this on camera. We had not come with spy equipment. But you don't always need a hidden camera to do a sting operation!

'Suku, we'll tell them that we are tourists doing a documentary on faith healing.'

'What if they recognise you?'

'It's a risk we take. I can always deny that I'm the TV chap.'

So out came the big beta camera with all the cables and microphone except the Star News collar.

The man in charge bought the story and with pride in his eyes began to show us around. After a round of deliberate inconsequential questions, I brought up the issue of people in chains.

'They will get violent and we need to chain them to control them. That is why they are so calm now.'

'But isn't that cruel? Remember, what happened here last year?'

'That was a freak incident. Fires don't break out every day. There is no other way to keep them here.'

It took some effort for the 'tourist' to digest these outrageously casual remarks. Masking my anger was quite a task. But I knew I had to play along to put out this story.

After politely turning down the manager's offer of lunch, I shot a piece to camera from the site of last year's blaze, where, quite shockingly, there were still pieces of cloth and burnt wooden logs strewn around.

'Suku, everything is recorded, right?' I wanted to ensure that Murphy's Law was not in operation!

We headed straight to the Ramanathapuram Collectorate.

There is a Tamil saying. 'Even if God is willing to give you a boon, the *pujari* will not!' Many government offices, particularly the ones away from State capitals may as well display this.

Here the only board read: S.Vijaykumar, IAS, Collector.

He was an affable officer whom I had met on an earlier occasion. Only this time, his P.A. decided to throw his weight around, probably annoyed by the prospect of his afternoon siesta being ruined by a TV crew.

So he chose to tell us that the Collector was having a nap!

My mobile phone battery was almost dead. I was equally drained out. My soles were burnt walking inside that 'shelter', and my stomach was growling.

'Can I charge my phone here?'

'Get the Collector's permission.'

'I need to call him as you are not sending my card inside. That's why I need to charge my phone. I will charge it only while making the call, just for a minute, even less…'

I went ahead as the P.A. picked up a Tamil magazine.

Surprisingly, the Collector picked up the call in three rings.

'Hi boss, sorry to bother you in the midst of your nap. Sanjay Pinto here from Star News.'

'Hi Sanjay. What nap?! I'm going through files.'

'Oh ok. That's what your P.A. told me! Can I come in?'

'Where are you?'

'Right outside your door!'

'Please, please. Come right in…'

The P.A.'s bell rang.

'*Ayya, seri ayya. Ippo Thaan Saar Vandhar.*' (Sir, ok sir. Sir came just now)

'Sanjay! How are you? Official trip here?'

'Totally! Doing a story on the Erwadi anniversary.'

'Great. We have done a lot of work after that incident. You may have read about our initiatives.'

'Yes, I have. Has chaining of inmates stopped?'

'We have given out a clear warning to all shelters to desist from such practices.'

I stopped short of giving the Collector the specific instance I had recorded.

As a journalist, this was my predicament. Telling him would obliterate my story. On the other hand, an uproar once the report was telecast would ensure that a State-wide raid was ordered and such crude practices were eradicated.

I mailed my script to Arnab that evening.

'Shocking. Are our visuals strong enough to establish this?'

'Yes.'

Predictably, the report sent the district administration into a tizzy. Star News wasn't available in Ramanathapuram at that time. So calls from the Health Secretary's office must have made Vijaykumar curse me. I felt sorry for him. He was a sincere officer who had been doing good work but evidently this place had clearly escaped his attention. I was just doing my job.

Raids were ordered and the chains removed.

Then, something really strange happened. A newspaper carried a damage-control report the next day, referring to the chains as 'decorative pieces on the ankles'.

Was the correspondent just a poor fiction writer that he viewed thick iron chains as anklets (*kolusu* in Tamil)? As for my story, the medium was the message; because the camera does not lie.

11

'VISHY' WASHY ENCOUNTER!

JOURNALISM MAY BE LITERATURE in a hurry but is often also a frenzied race to learn the basics of what you've been assigned to cover. And I'm not talking of rocket science and all those launches in Sriharikota I would be sent to report on because Chennai was much closer to the Satish Dhawan Space Centre than Hyderabad. One of my big regrets in life was not learning chess and swimming. My wife Vidya and I still make plans for the pool but they are like those Five Year Plans, which are always in the future! Now interviewing a world chess champion without knowing anything about the game is one thing; making a few moves for the camera, quite another! But when the champion happens to be someone as unassuming as Viswanathan Anand and your school senior to boot, it should be a breeze. Right? Wrong!

Vishy, as we affectionately call him, was my school mate at Don Bosco, Egmore. A senior who has been most appropriately held up as a role model for every new batch of students, year after year, with every new title he would win and defend. Vishy belongs to the 1987 batch of Don Bosco; four years my senior. We didn't get to see much of him, except during exams, as he used to travel extensively. The school was admittedly a big support and would not just give him attendance but also re-schedule exams for him. One of our teachers, and former Assistant Headmaster, Michael Sundar would often recall: 'Vishy would never take privileges for granted. If he missed classes, he would work overtime to complete his notes and homework.'

So how could I take him for granted? The Sports Desk, headed by Gulu Ezekiel, son of renowned poet Nissim Ezekiel, gave me a clear brief. 'Do a special sit down with Anand. Begin the interview with a few moves on camera.' I was too embarrassed to tell Gulu that I didn't know a thing about chess! A few quickfire 'learn chess' books were of no help.

Cameraperson Srinivasan had elaborate plans to frame the interview. Honestly, it felt like it was the interviewer who was going to be framed! It was decided that I would wear a white shirt and black trousers (my law school attire anyway) and Anand would be requested to wear a black shirt and white trousers. At Anand's residence, the camera crew went about making a backdrop to resemble a chess board with black and white squares. Gosh, all this and my opening moves?

I finally mustered the courage to confide in Anand that I knew zilch about chess and that we had to shoot this terrifying opening move. He patted me on the back and said: 'Hey, don't worry. We'll manage.'

As the camera rolled, I have no idea what pieces I moved but all that I remember was that Pinto was knocked down pronto! On air, my zero knowledge of chess didn't show. I had done my homework on the questions to salvage the rest of the shoot.

After the interview, we usually chat with the interviewee. Anand and I turned our attention to Don Bosco. I recalled an incident while playing the Don Bosco patented sport – crocker (half cricket, half baseball, with a half out!). A juicy full toss on my leg stump was way too tempting to resist pulling over mid-wicket. The ball landed on Anand's bench and missed his lunch box full of curd rice by a whisker. I was ordered by the bowler to get the ball back. With considerable trepidation, I walked up to Anand and even before I could apologise, he gave me the ball and said: 'Hey nice shot. Sorry you missed a four because of me.' He obviously didn't know my name but we all knew him, as the world chess champion.

Frankly, for a school that was better known for State ranks, cricket and table tennis, to make a mark in a relatively less glamorous sport like chess, called for nothing short of world class standards. Just into his teens, Vishy was World No. 3 in the sub-junior category. Well before the newspapers had pictures of the State Toppers in the Class 10 exam, Vishy made headlines as the Government of India had decided to honour this 15-year-old student with the Arjuna award for being an 'Outstanding Sportsperson'.

The laurels kept flowing in and no quiz competition was ever complete without a question or two on Vishy's latest victories! Talking of quiz contests, I must tell you about Vishy's 'disqualification' from a competition in the Philippines! As this boy wonder was collaring every prize for solving the most complicated puzzles, the organisers asked him to stop participating! The prizes were books. So they told Vishy to take as many books as he could possibly carry but to give the others a chance!

Though he comes across as serious in interviews, I for one know that Anand is very different with his family and friends. Anand's mother and first coach, the late Susheela Aunty (God bless her soul), used to chuckle whenever she would remember a prank Anand had played on her in Spain many years ago. He had taught her a few mischievous words in Spanish and the poor lady got to know about the real meaning only after trying it out on her maid!

We've all heard of alumni going back as Chief Guests to their Alma Mater. Anand was one of the few students to have been invited as a Guest of Honour at the Independence Day function when he was in Class 12. I still vividly admire this affable senior sitting on the stage in a striped T-shirt, next to his father, who incidentally was the General Manager of Southern Railways and the Chief Guest that year.

My last interview with Anand was in 2012 after he was crowned 'World Champion' for the fifth time. We chatted briefly, yet again about our old school, as cameraperson Sukumar took what we call 'cut away shots' in TV jargon.

'I'm planning to attend the silver jubilee of my 1987 batch in August', he said quite excitedly.

We later bumped into each other at Vruksha Play school where my kids – Sanvi and Vidan – ended up as his son Akhil's classmate. Soon, other championships beckoned and he was off to win more laurels. When I pinged his wife Aruna, also a good friend, asking if Anand would mind giving me a short take on my stint with NDTV for my maiden book on public speaking, what I got was touching: Anand recalled my human interest stories, not our wishy-washy chess encounter!

12

BRAVEHEART'S MOTHER

THE KARGIL WAR SERVED as a big learning curve and an opportunity to the media in terms of war coverage. Some of my colleagues from Delhi who covered the war, not as embedded journalists but on their own, sleeping behind rocks and reporting stories of courage and sacrifice of our soldiers, were privileged. Back in the bureaus, we got to focus on the grief and mourning of families who lost their brave sons, brothers and husbands. When a coffin, wrapped in the tricolour, is brought home, it is impossible to hold back tears.

In May 1999, Major M. Saravanan, the son of an Army IPKF veteran A. Mariappan, was assigned the task of capturing a fortified Pakistani position: Point 4268 in the Batalik region of Kargil at a height of over 14,000 feet. It was a risky challenge as the enemy troops had a distinct advantage of being at a much higher altitude. Our brave Indian *jawans* engaged the adversaries for almost three hours and Major Saravanan killed a couple of them. In the exchange, Major Saravanan fell to enemy shelling. His body was recovered about a month later.

A pall of gloom descended on his home in Trichy in Tamil Nadu. I was sent to cover the arrival of the braveheart's body. It was heart breaking to hear stories of the young officer's childhood passion for the army from his family and friends who had gathered. I wanted to get a short interview with his mother Amrithavalli. Of course, unlike some in the media, I was most definitely not going to parrot that insensitive, silly poser: 'How do you feel?' On such occasions, you don't even need to ask questions. Just sit with them and allow them to open up. If she was willing to speak, I would have asked her to tell us a little about her darling son. I went up to Mrs. Mariappan. As soon as I offered my condolences, she burst into tears and rushed into one of the rooms. I was moved and shaken. Her grief was obviously too much to bear. To bury your own child is the worst nightmare of any parent.

I waited outside till one of Major Saravanan's sisters called me in. I cannot recall if it was the elder or younger sibling; Revathi or Chithra. During a short interview on how her brother was always so protective, kind and generous, I was choked with emotion. I prayed for the family and left. Throughout my journey back to Chennai, the image of the grieving mother breaking down kept coming back. I hardly spoke to the cameraperson.

On reaching Chennai, I confided in Jennifer Arul, my senior colleague and Bureau Chief. With a mother's instinct, she responded. 'Sanjay, I should have gone instead. You probably reminded her of her son.' I guess Jennifer was right. I was 26 years old, exactly the age of the Vir Chakra awardee. In the hustle and bustle of news, these are things you never really factor in. It taught me a lesson in sensitivity that I will never forget.

The sense of sacrifice that defence families are known for is inspiring as it is moving. A decade after his martyrdom, the Mariappans had in place the Major Saravanan Memorial Trust and were in the thick of a drive to motivate youngsters to join the Army. I never had the honour of meeting the Hero of Batalik but when I stand at attention when the national anthem is played, the image of that grieving mother's face often comes right back.

I salute the memory and sacrifice of Major Saravanan.

13

WAKE UP, MR. MINISTER!

AS A FIFTEEN-YEAR-OLD school boy, I was quite fascinated by the job of a detective; shadowing, snooping and barging in when you need to. So irrepressible was my desire, that my father sent me to meet a private sleuth who had put out an advertisement in the *Indian Express*, offering free detective coaching for lawyers, students, housewives, even police officers! Armed with a testimonial from Police Commissioner P. Dorai, whose son Raajiv was my classmate in school, I attended the interview at the office on Mount Road and got selected.

A maiden assignment involved travelling to Rameshwaram where a 35-year-old man was suspected to have been murdered in a lodge, but a suicide case had been registered by the local police. My parents felt it was too risky for a boy of my age and shot down the idea. My detective dream was soon shelved as exams took over. But the spark was not extinguished.

Six months into my job as a Chennai Correspondent of NDTV, Star News, I had to track down a Union Minister. The AIADMK was an integral part of the BJP-led National Democratic Alliance and had a sizeable representation in the Cabinet. Kadambur Janardhanan, an elderly party man and staunch Jayalalithaa loyalist, who would stand out in any crowd with the generous amount of vermillion smeared on his forehead, was the Minister for Personnel. This was a key portfolio as several sensitive departments like the Enforcement Directorate came under his sway.

A controversial move that made national headlines was the Centre's order transferring the Enforcement Director M.K. Bezbaruah. This was bang in the middle of the officer's investigation into the Jain *hawala* and godman Chandraswami cases. Apparently, the file was signed without keeping the Personnel Minister in the loop. Jayalalithaa would have none of this and promptly demanded the reinstatement of Bezbaruah in the national interest.

'Sanjay dear, Janardhanan is not in Delhi. He must be somewhere in Chennai. Get him, please. We need his reaction desperately.' That was Barkha Dutt on the phone.

'Will try, Barkha.'

'Try' is a prophylactic expression very commonly used by young reporters to buy a little breathing space!

Where do I begin my hunt for this man? What if he is enjoying a massage at Fisherman's Cove! Weird thoughts crossed my mind.

'Let me first eliminate the most obvious possibilities,' I thought to myself. The first stop was the AIADMK Headquarters in Royapettah.

Mahalingam, the office manager was busy faxing press releases.

'Mahalingam Sir, where is Kadambur *Ayya*?' (a Tamil suffix to denote respect)

'No idea.'

None of the other party workers had a clue.

Step two was quite laborious. I started calling all the star hotels in the city. That's where most of the Union Ministers who don't have homes in Chennai stay.

These are probably tricks they don't teach you at Journalism College!

'Hello, connect me to Mr. Kadambur Janardhanan, please. Central Minister staying here. It's urgent.'

I was merely shooting in the dark and confidently at that!

I made more than a dozen calls but drew a blank.

Something made me dial the State Guest House in Chepauk, opposite the M.A. Chidambaram cricket stadium. 'Hello, at what time did the Minister check in? Kadambur Janardhanan.'

'Hello, sir. Sir, arrived half an hour back. Who is speaking sir?'

Why alert the blokes by answering that!

Our driver Mohamed got us there in 10 minutes. We didn't drive in. Instead, we parked the car away from the main gate. At the porch, the official car with a red beacon was a giveaway. I asked cameraman Prakasam to go in and check which room had men in white *veshti*s hanging around. I didn't want to risk identification by going in myself. Prakasam returned in 5 minutes quite excited.

'First floor *yaar.* I heard some of them talking about going out for lunch to the MLAs canteen.'

'Brilliant. Let's wait here. If the Minister accompanies them, we catch him at the canteen. Otherwise, without most of his minions, we can sneak into his room!'

Luck favours the street smart guy! The entire group left to have lunch.

I called the Guest House. The phone kept ringing.

'Hey, it looks like the receptionist has also gone for lunch!'

Prakasam and I slunk in and went up to the first floor. I knocked at the slightly ajar door. No response. We decided to enter the suite. In an adjoining room was our man, fast asleep and snoring quite loudly! There is always a certain level of brashness that goes with a rookie journalist. Instinctively, I went inside and cleared my throat. No response!

'Sir,' I said gently, as I patted his hand.

Janardhanan woke up, looking justifiably startled.

'Who are you? What do you want? Where have these fellows gone?'

'Sanjay Pinto, Star News. Your men just went for lunch! Need to do an interview urgently on the Bezbaruah transfer. What sir, they didn't consult you or Madam?'

'Leave me. How can they not get Amma's opinion; our party leader's opinion? We are their ally; very bad.'

'Indeed, sir. Can I record your comments, please?'

'Wait, let me wash my face.'

'You look fine, sir. Just adjust your hair!'

Janardhanan was evidently an extremely unassuming Minister! I finished the interview in less than 5 minutes.

'Did you have lunch? Shall I order *sambar* rice for you?'

'No sir, thanks. I need to send this to Delhi immediately. Thank you, sir.'

My sound bite was far more important than lunch!

'Hello, Barkha! Got him! Says it's against coalition *dharma*... Uplinking in 15 minutes.'

14

THOUSAND LIGHTS TO DALLAS

IN A STATE WHERE film stars eventually change their stripes, making the leap from the box office to the ballot boxes seem like a casual swagger, every election is a blockbuster. The cut outs, the posters, the slogans, the fiery speeches punctuated with personal jibes, the costumes of street dancers and the blaring film music with improvised lyrics: the colours of an election campaign in Tamil Nadu are unbeatable. To capture that setting and flavour, garnished with exclusive tête-à-têtes with the bigwigs in the fray, was the brief any serious political correspondent would carry.

'The DMK's generation next, Karunanidhi's heir apparent, M.K. Stalin and his pocket borough, Thousand Lights.'

That was the assignment mailed by my Political Editor Rajdeep Sardesai. It was meant to be a half-hour 'Constituency Profile' in a walkabout fashion.

(I once couldn't resist doing a fun piece on Stalin's speculated hair job in Bangkok and calling it 'hair apparent'!)

Unlike the North, the access journalists usually get in Tamil Nadu to political leaders on the campaign trail is depressingly negligible. You can't play Hamlet without the Prince of Denmark. Neither could I have showcased the electoral battle of the DMK Commander (*Thalapathi* in Tamil) without exclusive interaction with him while canvassing votes. Stalin was an early riser and seldom missed his morning walk at IIT Madras. His campaign for the day usually started at 8 o'clock after a light breakfast of two *idlis* and *sambar*. After all, it made sense to reserve some space for the soft drinks and milk that his followers in the constituency would almost certainly cajole him into having along the way.

I tracked Stalin from the minute he stepped into his red modified open jeep. For an otherwise serious person, he smiled quite a bit whenever anyone waved to him from houses and apartments en route, or held aloft new born babies to be named. As the convoy passed a roadside temple, Stalin got off the vehicle and bowed as a priest did an '*arthi*'.

I followed closely and as he was about to get back onto the jeep, I quizzed him: 'Are you religious?'

'Not religious' was an almost instantaneous answer.

The DMK stands for rationalism and many in the party, right from M. Karunanidhi, are atheists.

This image was an interesting aside, although the VIP contestant played down any significance.

Thousand Lights is a Muslim-dominated area. With the DMK's consistent pro-minorities stance, winning was not a worry for Stalin. At one stop, a glittering sword was presented to the party boss's son with a crown, as slogans hailing him as the inheritor of Karunanidhi's political legacy drowned the film music in the background. He raised the sword, unable to suppress a boyish smile!

This, I felt, was the right time to 'strike'. I walked up to Stalin and thrust my mike forward.

'Are you Karunanidhi's political heir?'

'Who says that? Gopalsamy?' he shot back, referring to his old rivalry with MDMK Chief Vaiko who was called V. Gopalsamy when he was in the DMK.

'No, I am asking you that. Moreover, your father has all along been saying that you have all the qualities to take on the DMK chief's mantle some day.'

'We are a democratic party. Such decisions are taken at the General Council. I am not after posts.'

'You also hold the post of Youth Wing President, but you will soon become a grandfather!'

Stalin smiled. One of his followers who was within ear shot, asked me, 'Does he look like a grandfather?'

My honest reply was: 'No. But isn't my question valid?'

'Our *Thalapathi* is youthful in his looks and in his thinking. So there is no issue.'

The convoy moved on. I had enough for a colourful episode. But we continued to follow him till the end of the day.

Editing a half-hour late into the night after a gruelling day in the sun was what a typical election season day often turned out to be.

I mailed the next day's plan with a footnote – 'Stalin Walkabout uplinked at 2.30 am. Will be in office by 11 am' – in order to dispense with the customary morning call from the Input Desk.

By the time I got home, it was 3 in the morning. I was too tired to even change my clothes and crashed into bed with my socks on.

Good sleep is any night better than wealth. But if you're a 24x7 journalist, you do need to be prepared for those onerous 'sorry for the interruption' wake-up calls at ungodly hours. Three hours into my deep slumber, the siren went off. That was the ring tone on my mobile! This time it had nothing to do with work. My mother was on her way to the United States for a family reunion and was scheduled to land around 6 a.m. IST. I answered the phone like the symbol of justice, with my eyes closed and ears open, expecting my mother to confirm her safe arrival at the Dulles Airport in Washington DC.

It was my Uncle Tony Henry on the line.

'Hey Sanjay. Tony here. Where's your Mom?'

'Oh God, Tony. I'm almost sleep-talking; got to bed at 3 o'clock. Can we joke later, please?'

'Sanjay, I'm not joking. Your mom is not on the flight. We waited till the last passenger got off and checked with the airline staff. Her name is not on the passenger manifest. Where is she?'

That's when my eyes opened.

'What are you saying, Tony? I had her escorted right up to the aircraft. She even called me after being seated inside just before the take off. How can she not be on that flight? What has happened?'

'Very strange, Sanjay; can you get in touch with the police there?'

'Sure. Rightaway.'

I called my friend Surya Prasad, Deputy Commissioner of Police, Airport Security & Anti Hijacking. Surya's office had helped my mother at the Airport while she checked in.

Surya was on a treadmill at the gym at Hotel Ambassador Pallava.

'Hi Sanjay. Has Aunty reached?'

'No boss. Something has happened...'

'Wait a sec.'

(Surya stopped the treadmill)

'Is she ok?'

'We don't know where she is, boss.'

'Meaning? My boys put her on the flight. Every passenger has to be accounted for. Let's check at the connecting flight point. I'll ask my officers to do that. Give me a few minutes. I'll call you back.'

After Surya hung up, I called the travel agent. He didn't pick up.

My mother usually flies British Airways: Chennai-London – London-Washington.

As I was busy with the election, I didn't check her ticket that was sent by the agent based on my mother's booking instruction

I kept trying the agent. After ten minutes, he finally answered sounding quite groggy: 'Good morning Sir. Sorry, I had a late night. I went to bed only at 11.30 pm.'

'Not a very good morning Mr. Hariharan. I didn't have a late night. I've had an early morning. Anyway, my mother hasn't reached the Washington Airport. It seems her name is not on the list either.'

'But sir, she will land only in the afternoon. And you said Washington?'

'Afternoon? Excuse me. The flight has landed there. Yes, Washington. Why?'

'Just a second, Sir. Let me recheck my file.'

(Returns in 2 minutes. The longest I've experienced, as strains of *suprabatham* could be heard in the background.)

'Sir, she hasn't gone to Washington. She told me she had to go to Dallas! That's what we booked her on.'

'Mr. Hariharan. My mother is sixty years old. She knows the address of her family there. Why would she go to Dallas? She has no one there. All her brothers and sisters are in Virginia, near Washington.'

'But sir, she clearly told me Dallas.'

Here was the catch. Diction and pronunciation are not the best when it comes to the average booking agent. My mother had mentioned the name of the Airport in Washington DC: 'Dulles'! Mr. Hariharan took that for Dallas.

I called my uncle back.

'Tony, there has been a terrible mix up. She is on her way to Dallas. The agent, actually mum also, goofed up. The chap heard Dulles as Dallas!'

'Sanjay, that's halfway across the country from Washington DC the other end of town! Let me find out when that flight lands.'

'Ok Tony. Let me also check.'

Surya called back. I told him about the confusion.

'Yes. We had her name announced at the Airport but the connecting flight to Dallas has taken off.'

As the agent said, the flight to Dallas was expected to land in about six hours. That would be well past midnight there. Imagine my mother, travelling alone and the type who would panic for the slightest reason, like missing a bus, landing at an odd hour in a foreign land with no relatives waiting for her at the Airport. My priority was to prevent a panic attack. I had five hours to do that.

Tony called back.

'Sanjay, we've got her a connecting flight from Dallas to Washington. The ticketing has been done. But it's only tomorrow morning, our time.'

'Oh ok. So she has to check into a hotel for the night when she lands?'

'Yes, we are arranging for that too.'

'Great, but she will definitely get hysterical.'

I rang Surya again.

'Sorry boss to be disturbing you like this…'

'Shut up *yaar*. What are friends for?'

I told him about my concern.

'Oh that's all? Don't worry. We can handle that. Leave it to me. Go back to sleep now!'

'Whaaat? How?'

'My nephew Krishna lives in Dallas. I will call him now and explain everything. He will go to the Airport, receive Aunty and take her home. The next morning she will be put safely on the flight to her real destination!'

'Goodness gracious. As simple as that? Thanks a million, boss. I owe you one! Can you give me Krishna's number please?'

I had a word with Krishna. He seemed very friendly.

'Yes, Uncle gave me the lowdown! I'll be there. Don't worry. I'll call you.'

Tony buzzed again. I briefed him. There was a collective sigh of relief.

As all the drama was unfolding, the best part was that the passenger was blissfully unaware that she was on a wrong flight!

My eyes were closing. I dozed off in a few minutes.

By the time I woke up it was 1 p.m.!

It was such a sound sleep that I didn't hear a string of calls.

'Hello Krishna, Sanjay here! Has my mother landed?'

'Yes, Sanjay. We tried calling you. She is asleep now. Will get her to call you when she wakes up.'

'Thank you Krishna. You are a Godsend.'

The school teacher that my mother was, had learnt the biggest lesson of her life. Or so I believed! When she called, she was furious and wanted to sue the travel agent.

'It's not his fault, *ma*. You should have given the name of the place, not the airport! If you book a ticket from Chennai to Delhi, would you say "I want to go to Indira Gandhi"?'

15

ELOQUENT SILENCE

HINDI WAS MY SECOND language in school. I 'studied', rather struggled with, it for twelve years. It was my father's idea that I should learn a language that would help me if I were to land a job in North India. There was something fundamentally wrong with the teaching of the language in my school. While my vocabulary was reasonably good, my grammar was just all over the place. Hindi examinations meant memorising poems, long essays, and explanation of verses. At the end of twelve years of study, I could, in five minutes, rattle off a printed page of Hindi verbatim, but could not carry on a grammatically correct conversation for more than three sentences.

Little did I realise that a decade after passing out of school, I would have to address the nation in Hindi. And live at that! Those were the days when English bulletins on Star News, which NDTV produced, used to be aired on the hour and Hindi news on the half hour. The Chennai Bureau did not have a Hindi

Correspondent though in many stations, the Reporters were bilingual. I clearly was not. For headline news developments, it was customary to get the Bureau Correspondents to do phone-ins in Hindi. When my headquarters came to know that I had studied the language for twelve years, they probably mistook me for a Hindi pundit!

I was at the Gopalapuram residence of DMK patriarch M. Karunanidhi. After many years, MDMK Chief Vaiko, who had formed the MDMK in 1996 after being shown the door by the DMK, was all set to meet his former mentor and *Annan* (elder brother), to join a political alliance in Tamil Nadu. It was a classic return of the Prodigal Son story and assumed national interest.

The video cameras rolled and the still cameras clicked away as Vaiko walked in to 'Kalaignar Illam' (Karunanidhi's home). The meeting lasted about an hour. Known for his way with words, Karunanidhi was asked if it was a historic meeting, given the acrimonious parting of ways over in the past, when Vaiko had accused the DMK of promoting dynastic politics. The grand old man quipped: 'Today's news is tomorrow's history.' That was easily the headline of the day. Karunanidhi's one liners would make it to the front pages of newspapers with such regularity that if a press conference lasted more than 10 minutes, he would jocularly ask journalists: 'What, you still haven't found your headline?'

This was in the late nineties, before OB Vans came into the picture. Breaking news called for phone-ins. As the development was considered significant, especially in the context of how the DMK's heir apparent M.K. Stalin, whose promotion in the party was resented by Vaiko, would take it, the Hindi Desk in my head office pleaded with me to do a short Hindi phone-in. I initially put my foot down but an impassioned plea prompted me to reluctantly agree. Some of my senior colleagues in the profession, like K.N. Arun, who were fluent in Hindi and present at the spot, offered to help me with translating a few sentences in Hindi.

'All right, just one question. And I will read out the Hindi answer that I have jotted down.' That was the deal I had struck with the Hindi team in Delhi.

Kanupriya Sehgal, a former Miss India, was the Hindi anchor. I am pretty sure the desk forgot to apprise her of the 'deal'. In chaste Hindi, Kanupriya asked me a question. The only thing I could decipher were the names 'Vaiko' and 'Karunanidhi'! I stuck to my scribble. Just as I was about to pull up my collar, came a second salvo! Not only was this an egregious breach of the 'deal' but honestly, the question sounded like Greek or Latin to me! I had three choices. To blabber something in grammatically incorrect Hindi, to repeat the first answer (like I used to in my Hindi examinations!) or to keep silent. I chose the last option.

'Hello Sanjay, are you there? Sanjay, Sanjay...' I could hear Kanupriya anxiously trying to ferret out an answer.

I remained quiet. After a third attempt, I realised I was successful, when the anchor broke into the stock apology to the viewers 'I think we have lost the audio with Sanjay Pinto. We will try and connect with him again shortly.'

'Oh not a chance in hell', I muttered to myself!

As I hung up, I also cracked up. So did my other colleagues outside Karunanidhi's home when I narrated the 'adventure'.

Amused and miffed, I called the Hindi desk. Would you believe it; they actually believed that there had been an audio problem and had the gumption to ask if I was game for another phone-in!

The same evening, there was a development at the Raj Bhavan. My bureaucrat friends there brought up my Hindi phone-in. They too were as clueless as the Hindi desk and seemed surprised that I could speak Hindi 'so well' as an Aide-De-Camp to the Governor put it! I broke the news about my strategy and there were loud guffaws. When words fail you, so can the audio! Off the record!

16

WIRES CROSSED

IT'S A STANDARD TEMPLATE in the movies. The hero and heroine begin with a tiff, followed by a period of intense sulking, and from that misunderstanding, emerges a strong bond. News gathering encounters can easily mimic cinema.

Tamil Nadu is known for its accessible bureaucracy. The IAS and IPS tribe in the State are, by and large, not just helpful but friendly as well; unless you rub them the wrong way. A notable feature of the late Chief Minister Ms. Jayalalithaa's second innings was the relatively free hand she gave the police. Officers were carefully handpicked, based on their track record and inputs from veteran cops.

Fort St. George, the seat of power in the State, fell within the jurisdiction of the Flower Bazaar Deputy Commissioner of Police. The Secretariat was obviously the most important point in his daily beat. The officer had to receive the CM at the portico of the Secretariat with a salute every morning, and send her off in the afternoon or evening, depending on the engagements lined up. An insider revealed that the AIADMK supremo preferred a young and dynamic direct recruit IPS officer for this role. Mahesh Kumar Aggarwal, a 1994 batch officer was the chosen one.

At the time, Ms. Jayalalithaa was battling the slew of corruption cases filed against her by the previous DMK dispensation. The party, then in the opposition, had decided to implead in the TANSI land deal, which was a thorn in the CM's flesh. A television story, especially on NDTV, had to always present both sides. After a tip-off from my sources, I rushed from 'Anna Arivalayam', the DMK headquarters, to the Secretariat. The goal was to get Ms. Jayalalithaa to respond to the development.

In the age of 24x7 TV news, those in the corridors of power would always be tuned in and it was hardly difficult to predict why a TV crew was hanging around a particular place. If it was likely to be an inconvenient situation, the Public Relations Officers (PRO) of the government would be sent to dissuade the media from trying for an update or response. An ambush interview with the Chief Minister at the portico as she entered her car, was a PRO's nightmare. Actually, not just for the PRO, but the cops as well, as the entire lot would be pulled up in case anything went 'wrong'.

I was the only journalist who had landed up. Remember, this was when NDTV was one of the few private English national TV channels around. Splinter channels came a few years later. The local Inspector, Assistant Commissioner, and

CM's security personnel were unsuccessful in moving me away from the portico. This brought the young DCP to the spot. Mahesh Aggarwal looked like he was straight out of college! I had seen him in action when he was the Superintendent of Police, Theni, during the Parliamentary election. With a poker face, he requested me not to disturb the CM on her way out. I politely refused to walk away and stayed put.

When Ms. Jayalalithaa came downstairs towards her car, I called out to her.

'Good afternoon, Ma'am, I want your response to something, please.'

The security apparatus swung into action and tried to move me from the spot. In the melee, my microphone cable (well before the days of cordless mikes!) got entangled around the DCP!

The convent-educated CM was known to appreciate social graces.

'Good afternoon. What is it?'

'Ma'am, Mr. Karunanidhi says the DMK will implead in the TANSI case in the Supreme Court....'

Before I could complete the question, she shot back. 'The DMK always pursues vindictive politics. If Mr. Karunanidhi wants to implead, let him.' And she walked away, not too pleased with the development.

Ms. Jayalalithaa may have been an actor in her previous avatar but as a politician, she made no pretence about how she felt about news events. She seemed clearly miffed as she got into her car. I looked pleased with my effort as I had a story for the day. A balanced story at that.

After saluting his boss, D.C.P. Mahesh Aggarwal walked up to me and said sternly: 'What you did was not proper.'

Hardly a couple of years into my job, I was suitably brash and retorted. 'I did my job. You did yours.' Soon after the convoy left, I called Mrs. Gariyali, IAS, who was the Chief Minister's powerful Secretary with whom I had a good rapport. I wanted to get some information about another development and dialled her mobile number but it was on 'call waiting'. I did not even need to make a guess about who may have been on the line!

Mahesh left in his car, visibly upset. For the next few days, we both maintained a stony silence on seeing each other at the Secretariat.

A few weeks later, a common friend, Surya Prasad, another IPS officer, had invited me to his daughter's birthday party at a bowling point. Mahesh too turned up. We buried the hatchet over chocolate cake. At the time of writing, he is the Commissioner of Police of Madurai and one of my closest friends, a sort of elder brother, though only by a few months! The jury is still out on who played Big Brother that afternoon at the Secretariat Portico.

17

REVERSE SWING

PAID NEWS; PLANTED QUESTIONS; commercial plugs – authorised, accidental, or deliberate: all these were common in brand promotion. But a formal press meet with the organiser playing censor in an almost amusing fashion was not too common, to say the least.

'No questions on cricket, please. This is a strict brand promotion for Boost.' With that rider, a press conference with Sachin Tendulkar began at the Taj Coromandel Ballroom.

'Why did they call all journalists? They should have invited only food magazine writers or the Page 3 beat crowd.' Whispers could be heard from rows behind. Some journalists walked out in a huff. Others were calling their offices to check if they could boycott the event. And a few engineers from TV channels were seen removing the cables they had laid for live coverage of the interaction.

This was understandable. Even the hint of an answer from Sachin on his tennis elbow, or the use of a lighter bat, or the morale in the dressing room, or a new batting order would have made headlines. The diktat was quite like laying out a delicious buffet spread before a hungry band of foodies with an instruction not to touch anything except the *papad*s!

But then when a company splurges to sign up an international celebrity as big as Sachin, there has to be return on investment. But an 'embedded' press conference was certainly not the ideal way to go about it.

The first few questions, probably prompted by the corporate house, sounded like tailor-made advertising plugs. The lawyer in me had this habit of surfacing every now and then! I put up my hand. The cordless microphone was handed over to me by a public relations executive, sporting a smile as wide as the reception desk outside.

'A reminder to our media friends. Please confine yourselves to the product.'

I wonder why the reminder had to come just before my question.

'Sachin,' I began, 'how will your opening of the innings 'boost' the performance of Team India?'

The twist provoked laughter in the hall from almost everyone, including the corporate head honchos.

Sachin smiled but perhaps he didn't quite hear the question. Or he probably wanted a few more seconds to think.

'Can you repeat that, please?'

I complied.

Like he despatches a full toss over mid wicket, the little genius came back with a flourish.

'Boost is the secret of my energy.'

The laughter was much louder this time. The company officials were ecstatic that their tag line was so powerfully driven home by their costliest brand ambassador.

'No more bouncers, please.' This was Sachin's plea after the googly. As if on cue, there were more guffaws.

As he left the hall, Sachin patted me on the shoulder and said: 'Hey, good one. You almost stumped me!'

'Thanks Sachin. But you stuck to your crease incredibly well!'

18

DEAD OR ALIVE

UNLIKE POLICE STATIONS IN the country, 'jurisdiction' is never an issue among bureaus of 24x7 television news channels. As I was lining up a human interest story for Gandhi Jayanthi in 2003, my mobile rang. It was about 4:30 p.m.

'Sanjay, rush to Tirupati! Assassination attempt on Chandrababu Naidu. How fast can you get there?'

That was an Input Editor from the Delhi office as soon as the news first broke on the wires.

'I will leave right away. Tirupati is about 3 hours from Chennai.'

Although the temple town falls under the Hyderabad Bureau's jurisdiction, my counterparts there – Uma and T.S. Sudhir – were a good 580 kilometres away. As I was just 150 kilometres from ground zero, I was despatched! Yes, we are sometimes like postal covers with stamps pre-fixed (read: a packed bag always ready!)

Having had my baptism by fire – I had joined NDTV right after the serial blasts in Coimbatore targeting BJP leader L.K. Advani – a blast-aftermath related story didn't seem all that daunting. Not that I had a choice!

I have always hated road travel. Even as a little boy, I would throw up on most school excursions. My mother would send bottles of orange and lime juice with little slices of ginger to check the inevitable! As a TV hack, your channel would always wish you had Michael Schumacher as your driver! Our chap was not too bad and got us to the spot in about two and a half hours. The road was dusty and a burnt smell – from overheated clutch plates of the steady stream of vehicles – was hanging heavy in the air. As someone with a dust allergy, and being easily susceptible to throat infections, a handkerchief around my mouth seemed the only precaution I could take. My close-cropped hair, khaki trousers, brown boots and a sky blue shirt probably made me pass for an intelligence or crime branch sleuth! Sometimes it helped.

My first reaction on reaching the site of the blast was: 'How on earth did this man survive.' It just had to be a miracle, occurring as it did in the vicinity of the abode of Lord Balaji. The white bulletproof ambassador car was mangled almost beyond recognition. I couldn't help wondering if an ordinary car would have been reduced to a heap of ashes. The initial bits of information began to trickle in. It was a powerful claymore mine, placed under stones and set off by a camera flash gun. The Andhra Pradesh Chief Minister Chandrababu Naidu had been seated in the front seat next to the driver. So powerful was the impact of the blast that the car was hurled in the air and hit a boulder before toppling over.

What struck me was the unhindered access to the scene of crime. The ease with which the local journalists were able to work in what was actually a sterile area was worth a case study at police academies. The investigators merely checked the identities of the mediapersons and then let them be. My piece to camera was in front of the mangled car.

Disaster or crime coverage is never complete with just spot reports. Any editor would love to get something that the others don't have. My headquarters kept feeding me with updates that were slowly coming out on PTI and other sources. While the focus of the story was obviously the condition of the main target, Chandrababu Naidu, the medical progress of the others in the vehicle, like IT Minister Gopalakrishna Reddy, was also newsworthy. A news channel started running as 'Breaking News': 'IT Minister Reddy Succumbs to Blast Injuries.' Delhi called to share the news as I was just entering the Sri Venkateshwara Hospital where Naidu and the other injured were undergoing treatment.

A trick they never teach you at Journalism School (not sure if they teach you any tricks, actually!) is to confidently and hurriedly breeze through the entrance of any news hotspot, as if you are urgently wanted inside! This incidentally, is the same tactic you use to enter your friend's home where there is a ferocious dog waiting to pounce on you! There it is a matter of smell! Here it was a question of the urgency in your eyes. My priority was to check the 'breaking news' on the IT Minister.

I walked into the ICU holding my NDTV mike like a torch, only to spot someone waving to me. Guess who! Now I wasn't sure if the channel in question believed in reincarnation! But Gopalakrishna Reddy had spotted the mike logo and recognised my face. So here I was speaking exclusively to the man another channel had almost put out an obituary on! Reddy didn't say much, obviously, but managed a few answers, enough to convince the world that he was miraculously alive.

I called my Input Desk. 'Hi. Do dead men talk?'

'What? Sorry.'

'Ok, my mobile phone battery is dying. Let's chat later. The IT Minister is alive; he has a few fractures. I've got him on camera.'

Buoyed by this exclusive, I even gave Naidu's room a shot but the security officials told me that he was asleep. I had no reason to believe otherwise, after what the poor TDP leader had been through.

A mere exclusive interview is hardly enough for a big story like this. In TV journalism, you can't afford to rest on your exclusives.

Delhi called that night. 'What's your day plan for tomorrow? Sonia suggests that you follow the investigation into the blast.'

'Sure; will file a story by the evening.'

I headed to the spot after breakfast. Top Andhra Pradesh CID officials were combing the area. I quietly followed them around. Again no questions asked. An advantage with working for a national network is that you are recognised even outside your usual place of work. More claymore mines were detected.

The sleuths then stumbled upon a long patch of grass leading to the stones under which the claymore mines were placed by the Peoples War. A horticulturist was roped in to zero in on the approximate age of the blades of grass. It soon became evident that the attack had been planned a few months in advance, exploiting the gaps in Naidu's security apparatus: dysfunctional metal detectors, the absence of jammers and no convoy of identical cars with the same registration numbers to hide the real vehicle in which the VIP travels.

This was certainly no scoop but a mere 'tell it like it is' investigation update, thanks to a team of very cooperative CID sleuths who realised that we were just doing our job by observing them doing theirs.

Uma and Sudhir called that evening.

'Congrats Sanjay. Good work.'

It always feels good to get a pat on the back from credible colleagues.

'Thanks. I guess your reputation in your State helped! Not to forget, my cameraperson's help, my cop like appearance (!) and the smattering of 'Beginners Level' Telugu I learnt at Loyola College.'

And with Naidu back in Hyderabad with a fractured collar bone and his wife promising to donate her *mangalsutra* to Lord Balaji, it was time to say, as we did on our 'Southern Edition' episodes (a great programme that was sadly scrapped) 'Back to you, Sudhir.'

19

'SOUND' BITE!

A THORN IN THE flesh of two neighbouring States – Tamil Nadu and Karnataka – the Veerappan saga seemed like a movie with no ending. The Sathymangalam forest brigand was known to be ruthless, his 'Robin Hood' image in some quarters notwithstanding. So when the Tamil sandalwood smuggler abducted Kannada matinee idol Rajkumar, who had a massive fan following in Karnataka, the two State governments had a law-and-order issue on their hands. Efforts to nab the fugitive had drawn a blank, forcing the states into a negotiation, with a vernacular journalist sporting a matching moustache playing emissary.

One of Veerappan's demands for the release of his VIP hostage was the setting free of 121 TADA detenus in Karnataka and five in Tamil Nadu prisons. Section 321 of the Criminal Procedure Code empowered the State government to withdraw prosecution in public interest but subject to guidelines framed by the Supreme Court. As the release of the extremists was seen as a Hobson's choice, the files were signed and the decision communicated to the courts.

This is when Abdul Karim, a retired Deputy Superintendent of Police, whose son had been killed, allegedly by Veerappan's gang in a forest ambush in 1992, moved in to spoil the party. The senior citizen filed a Special Leave Petition in the Supreme Court, challenging the release of Veerappan's associates on the ground that several courageous officers like his son had laid down their lives in the fight against the outlaw and such a step by the two governments would send wrong signals and make elected establishments seem like soft states. A Supreme Court Bench found *prima facie* merit in the submission, and ordered an interim stay on the release of the detenus.

The news had just broken. For the Tamil Nadu government, this was a huge setback. So it was big national news. The DMK was in power and M. Karunanidhi in the hot seat. I was asked to get a response from the Chief Minister about the latest development. In a few minutes, I reached Karunanidhi's residence in Gopalapuram. The CM was about to leave for lunch at his other residence on Oliver Road. Probably aware of the possible question he would be asked, his camp office instructed the security to try and get me out of the place.

An inspector walked up to me.

'*Thambi* (an affectionate term in Tamil meaning younger brother) why are you standing here?'

'I need a reaction from the CM to the court stay order in the Veerappan case.'

'No, no, the CM does not wish to comment on the issue.'

As I refused to budge, a mild argument ensued.

'How do you know that already?'

'We have been instructed to ask you to leave.'

'But I'm not inside your house. I'm standing on the road!'

'This is a sterile zone. You cannot stand here without permission.'

'I don't need your permission, sir.'

'See, I'm doing my duty to inform you. Please leave now. You can try at the party headquarters in the evening.'

'I'm also doing my duty. I work for a 24-hour news channel, not a newspaper which comes out tomorrow that I can wait for so many hours to get a simple response to an issue of national interest. Please try and understand.'

'*Thambi*, the CM has to have lunch. Please cooperate.'

'I too have not had lunch. I will merely try my luck. If he speaks, fine. If he doesn't that's fine too.'

'You media people are so stubborn. You don't even respect elders.'

'You have no consideration for youngsters doing their job. We media people are not there to only come when we are called. News is what dictates our movement.'

With no sign of my leaving, Karunanidhi stepped out. The security blocked me. I was at least fifteen to twenty yards away. As he was getting into his car, I shouted out my question: 'Sir, how are you going to handle the Veerappan case now that the Supreme Court has stayed the release of TADA detenus?'

Karunanidhi stopped. He looked tired and upset. But he spoke briefly. I kept nodding. After a few seconds, he got into the car and sped away.

I called my head office and informed them about my exclusive sound bite. Just that I couldn't hear what he was saying. Inside the car, I asked the cameraperson for a headphone and switched on the camera. Guess what?! Karunanidhi hadn't answered my question. All that he said in Tamil had been: 'Don't you have some discipline? Some of you young journalists do not listen at all. You want instant reactions. I can't give you that. Naughty fellow.' Although Karunanidhi used to reprimand journalists sometimes, there was absolutely no rancour. It was more like a grandfather pulling up his grand kids.

I updated my office; they said, 'Can't you try again as he comes out after lunch?'

Who says youngsters don't listen?!

20

ARREST OF A PONTIFF

IN THE RUN UP to my birthday in mid-November 2004, I wasn't making party plans but working the phones over a vague clue about the impending arrest of a VVIP. I called the Inspector General of Police, North Zone, on the night of 11 November to get some clarity but he didn't answer calls on his mobile. I rang his residence landline and left a message. In hindsight, returning calls from a television journalist at a time when something big was brewing was clearly not a priority. Not calling back was also a clue that there was action ahead! These are signals one picks up in the rough and tumble of news gathering.

The next evening was Deepavali and the rumours gained momentum. It was close to midnight, when a police team from Tamil Nadu, led by senior police officers, including an Additional Director General of Police, landed at Chennai Airport, along with the Kanchi Shankaracharya Sri Jayendra Saraswati, head of the Kanchi Mutt. The high profile arrest sent the media into a tizzy. The Shankaracharya was not just a revered person in the country but also very influential in the corridors of power, both in the State and at the Centre. I had interviewed him once on his attempt to find an amicable solution to the Babri Masjid dispute. It was not actually an interview but more a message recorded on camera. As I was waiting to ask a few questions, a colleague, S. Anand from *Outlook* magazine, interrupted only to be reprimanded by the staff present in the room. The look on their faces suggested that it was sacrilege to stop the Seer in the middle of his speech. After the message, the Shankaracharya seemed relaxed; he chatted with us briefly and left the room.

Now, the case at hand was not some economic offence or tax matter but a murder charge on which he had been arrested. The manager of the Varadaraja Perumal Temple Shankar Raman had been hacked to death by a gang in the temple on the 3 September 2004, sending shockwaves across Kanchipuram. The police alleged that the Seer was part of the conspiracy to eliminate Raman. Shankaracharya looked tired and perturbed. The cops wanted him to get into a police van but he could be heard protesting: 'Am I sandalwood smuggler Veerappan to be taken in a police vehicle?' After a discussion, he agreed to step into a Tata Sumo and the convoy, including a large media contingent, headed straight to Kanchipuram, about 75 kilometres from Chennai, a drive of about an hour and a half.

Editorial calls at the headquarters can sometimes get the goat of correspondents on the field. Although we had great footage of what was obviously a big breaking story, someone in my Delhi office decided not to roll fresh bulletins around midnight. All that the night desk, which otherwise would hound you for 'forward plans, day plans and morning obs', conveyed to me was: 'Please be ready for the 6 am bulletin.' I protested. 'Viewers will see it all in the newspapers by then.' A few other channels went live that night. These are occasions when you can't help thinking of all the times references are made to what 'this channel is flashing or the news wires are saying'. I just had to lump it. But how could I not remember Lord Tennyson's 'Charge of the Light Brigade', that seemed so appropriate for reporters on the field: 'theirs not to reason why...'

None of us in the media could sleep that night. At about 5 a.m., the Shankaracharya was taken to the Magistrate. The Kanchipuram Superintendent of Police, Davidson Devasirvatham, a senior of mine at Loyola College and an officer of the highest integrity (I didn't know him then), denied the media permission to watch the court proceedings. There was an argument between Walter Scott of Press Trust of India (PTI) and Davidson over the refusal. 'Are you willing to go on record? Can we quote you?' he asked angrily. Davidson retorted: 'Yes.' Usually, the press is allowed inside court halls but security reasons were cited this time.

The court proceedings were wrapped up and the Seer was remanded to judicial custody. It marked the beginning of several twists and turns in the case. There are news developments that don't end with a story or a couple of follow-up reports but keep developing over several months. This was one of them.

The Kanchi Mutt had, and continues to have, devotees who constitute the *crème de la crème* of all professions. Law was most definitely one of them. The intellectual brahmin community came together with formidable legal firepower. I saw the tense look and pain in their eyes. Some of them were my friends. One of them was from a respected family of lawyers, whose mother-in-law later went on to be elevated to the Bench as a judge. Ram Jethmalani, the country's top criminal defence lawyer was engaged to argue the Seer's bail application, which was taken up on a Saturday in the Madras High Court by Justice R. Balasubramaniam. It was a predictably packed court hall. During this pre-CISF access-control period, any member of the public, not just the litigants, could walk in. I managed to jostle my way up to the front. Jethmalani preceded his arguments with two lines. 'I don't want to take up too much time. Because Your Lordship is busy. And so am I.' Justice Balasubramaniam, known to be patient and affable, smiled. 'The Acharya cooks his own food,' Jethmalani thundered, as he went on to argue that there was no question of a revered person of his stature and following ever being a flight risk. Despite the vociferous submissions, bail was denied. Ultimately, it was an erudite and soft spoken Chennai Lawyer Mr. Sathyanarayana (now Justice Sathyanarayana) who was successful in getting the Shankaracharya bail.

Davidson was transferred and Prem Kumar, a promotee officer was posted as the Superintendent of Police of Kanchipuram. After his release on bail, the Shankaracharya chose to stay in Kalavai, a small town about 45 kilometres, and a little over an hour's drive, from the Kanchi Mutt. He was observing a self-imposed vow of silence. Most of us in the Media had to camp here. There were no hotels in the vicinity. Most of us were famished. A colleague from Aaj Tak, Imran Quereshi finally managed to locate a small joint that was serving hot rice and sambar. I could not leave my OB Spot and by the time my live report ended, the food was over. The priests at Kalavai and the devotees who had gathered there were most thoughtful. Sensing our plight, they invited us for a simple but tasty vegetarian meal that I wolfed down with gratitude.

While I was licking my fingers, 'news' had leaked that the Seer had 'confessed' to the crime during custodial interrogation earlier. With my legal background, I was skeptical and did not take it seriously, as any confession made to a police officer is inadmissible as evidence. However, a few TV channels aired the development as 'breaking news' and in an age of copycat journalism, all hell broke loose. I stood my ground. That my Political Editor at the time – Rajdeep Sardesai – was also trained as a lawyer, and had impeccable news sense helped. I explained the legal position to Rajdeep and he immediately agreed to give what would not stick in court a pass.

The Kancheepuram S.P. who filed the chargesheet was considered a hard nut. But he seemed to have a clear understanding of how the media worked, especially the battle of perception, and was in control of the optics of the whole case as it unfolded. Armed with a 1800-page chargesheet, he also came prepared with a juicy, almost sensational sound bite, that most TV channels used as a 'breathe' in the headline: a production technique of playing the crux of a sound bite right after the headline text is read out by the anchor. 'It's Lord Varadaraja Perumal Vs Kanchi Shankaracharya', he thundered, before marching into the court room.

The Police proceeded full throttle with the investigation that saw many leaks to the media. One such story was about a mystery lady called Usha, whom the police claimed was the recipient of monetary remittances from the Mutt. A source got in touch with me and arranged a one-on-one interview with her. Usha turned out to be a cancer survivor who had been deserted by her husband and was receiving financial support from the Mutt. My interview, in which she maintained that she shared a pure *Guru-Shishya* relationship with the Seer, caused a mild flutter in the Madras High Court Press Room as many television journalists were flooded with calls from their headquarters after my story broke. This was because the police had claimed that she was absconding. That scoop had a flip side. The Intelligence sleuths who used to keep a tab on sensitive court proceedings began to hover around me inside court halls, just to ensure that I wasn't going to be privy to some other dollop of information, without their knowledge! Those were the years when I was much younger and more fired up, which I must confess, tends to wear out as you grow older.

The trial saw 189 witnesses being deposed, of which almost half of them turned hostile. This included the approver in the case. The Shankaracharya petitioned the Supreme Court that a free and fair trial was not possible in Tamil Nadu due to the vitiated atmosphere and the case was transferred to neighbouring Puducherry. In the trial that ensued over four years, the Public Prosecutor was changed and four judges heard the case, over countless adjournments. The national media lost interest in the case after a point, with the news cycle leading with developments in other parts of the country, until, of course, the acquittal of both the Senior and Junior Shankaracharyas and all the remaining 21 accused, of all charges in November 2013. By this time, I had made a shift from the newsroom to the courtroom and watched the news reports on television.

The Kanchi Trial taught me a lesson. It takes all kinds to make a world. Although I was fair and balanced in my coverage, a local politician attributed motives to the coverage at a public meeting, referring to the different religions of correspondents in the Chennai Bureau. I wish he had cited specific instances of bias or incorrect reportage; because there were none. A viewer spewed venom in the comments section of *ndtv.com*, with a wish that I be handed over to the KGB! I was the one who dug my heels in and refused to report the so-called 'confession' of the Seer to the cops. I was the one who dented the claim about that mystery woman beneficiary of Mutt money. A person who can vouch for all that today is none other than Shankaracharya's defence lawyer Mr. K.S. Dinakaran. Erudite and polite, he was affectionate towards me, ending every conversation with 'God Bless you'. I cherish my association with him. He once helped me with an exclusive interview with one of his American clients who was a victim of a crime in the city.

Truth be told, I was more careful reporting this trial than any other, because I knew that shooting the messenger is a national pastime.

21

MIDNIGHT ARREST

HERE'S A NEW MURPHY'S LAW: If anything can be missed, it will. And thereby hangs a tale, tinged with regret.

It was 29 June 2001. Ms. Jayalalithaa was back as Chief Minister of Tamil Nadu for the second time. After a hard day's work, I was lying on my bed at home. Bogged down by a personal issue, I could think of nothing else. Work was the last thing on my mind. But schooled in the NDTV style of 24x7 journalism, my mobile phone was never switched off.

At about 11 p.m., my cell phone rang. A trusted source was on the line.

'The entire police force is being mobilized. Something big is brewing.'

'What is it likely to be?'

'Not entirely sure, but it looks like a big arrest is on the cards.'

My natural instinct would have been to jump out of bed, call for a camera crew and rush out to pursue the lead. Instead,

I called my colleague and former Loyola College mate Sunil Prabhu and shared the tip off with him. Logistically, Sunil was in a better position to get cracking immediately as he was just leaving the Chennai Press Club along with a few of our camerapersons and reporters from NDTV's Tamil bulletin 'Vijay Seidhigal', after playing badminton. So from the channel's point of view, the information was acted upon with alacrity and zero delay. Sunil and the team rushed to our NDTV Bureau in CIT Colony, Mylapore, grabbed the camera equipment, and whatever mobile phones were charging in the office, and headed out. After half an hour, Sunil called back to check if it was a genuine lead or a hoax. All I could tell him was that it came from a credible source and asked him to keep trying. True to his reputation of being persistent and dedicated, Sunil, whom I have always respected as a journalist, took over from there.

In a couple of hours, all hell broke loose. There was high drama at the Oliver Road residence of M. Karunanidhi. A police team had knocked on his door to arrest the DMK supremo in a flyover scam. When Karunanidhi's family members told the cops that he was asleep, they refused to back down and went upstairs. Sun TV managed to rustle up a camera unit in the nick of time and that is how the world got to see those visuals of Karunanidhi being lifted and dragged out of his home as a family member screamed: '*Ayyo*, they are killing him, they are killing him.'

The then Union Minister Murasoli Maran, who was in the vicinity, reached the spot. When he protested, he too was dragged away by a constable, despite revealing that he had a pacemaker. Another Union Minister T.R. Balu, went in search of his leader. One of the stops was the old Admiralty House which housed the State Crime Branch CID office. At the gate, a furious Balu could be heard telling the police sentry: 'Open the door! (sic) I am a Union Minister; open the door.' Soon, Balu was also arrested, allegedly for preventing police officers from performing their duty. As M.K. Stalin, Karunanidhi's son, had been the previous Mayor of Chennai, the flyovers were his brainchild and he was the next target.

All this happened between midnight and sunrise. The DMK leaders were taken to the residence of a judge in Tower Block, Kilpauk, to be remanded. I reached the judge's residence at about 5:30 a.m. Sunil and our camera crew had already broken the news, and NDTV was the first national channel to air the news.

As Karunanidhi was being driven to the Chennai Central Prison, Sunil and I followed the convoy. I was in the official NDTV car. Having gone on the shoot directly, Sunil was in his maroon Hyundai Santro. As we were almost adjacent to the White Ambassador in which Karunanidhi was seated, I tried to shove the mike at him in a desperate bid to get a sound bite. The former Chief Minister looked tired, obviously, but seemed willing to speak. But the cops were in no mood to allow that. I could hear Sunil shouting 'George, don't do this to me.' Sunil had apparently felt that S. George, the then Joint Commissioner of Police, Central Chennai, who was leading the convoy, was trying to cut him off from the line. George drove on.

At the Chennai Central Prison, images of a worried Kanimozhi sitting on the floor next to her father Karunanidhi were splashed all over the media. So was that sensational footage recorded by SUN TV of the arrest, that was generously shared by them with all media houses.

The politics over the arrest played out swiftly. The DMK was part of the BJP-led National Democratic Alliance. Predictably, there was pressure on the AIADMK Government to release Karunanidhi and the other top leaders.

By 6 p.m., the edited story was ready. It was rightly piloted by Sunil, who had worked hard through the night, with my inputs and piece to camera outside the prison. Sunil was so tired that he crashed for an hour on the carpet in the then Bureau Chief Jennifer Arul's glass cabin. Even his mobile phone battery had been drained. Dr. Roy had called and left a congratulatory message for Sunil. Frankly, he deserved it. For me, it was a career miss. But television is a team game and NDTV was on top of the story. I remember Jennifer sending out an email to the top bosses in the channel giving me credit for sharing the tip off with the team. It helped in some measure.

There was no dearth of opportunities to earn your spurs in a 24-hour news channel. A few months later, in August, as Jennifer was on leave, Sunil and I took turns to editorially helm the Tamil News Bulletins – 'Vijay Seidhigal' – aired on Vijay TV. The two of us worked well as a team. Although we were not the best of friends in Loyola College, Sunil and I shared a healthy professional rapport.

On 12 August 2001, when the DMK organised a massive protest march against the arrest of their leader in Chennai, I had the final word on the coverage. I had a gut feel that the rally would be eventful. The previous night, at the assignment meeting, I asked all our reporters and camerapersons to fan out at different points along the route. My instruction was simple. We will only focus on the DMK rally. This editorial role in the Tamil bulletins did not absolve me of my reporting responsibility to NDTV 24x7. This effectively meant that I had to scamper from the terrace of the bureau, which was the Live OB spot for NDTV 24x7 and back to the news floor of the Tamil bulletin almost every hour from the time the rally started that afternoon.

As I had predicted, it turned violent. There was a *lathi* charge, tear gas and police firing in which a few DMK workers were killed and journalist colleagues like B. Jayashree and Manish from Aaj Tak were assaulted by the police. On the Marina Beach, there were gory scenes of people being hacked at with sharp weapons, which only our team managed to capture. I was the first to report the police firing and death toll on NDTV 24x7. As I went back to the Tamil news floor, Kalanidhi Maran, who was my senior in school and college, called on my mobile to request a dump of the Marina Beach footage. I told him that I would have to check with my Head Office as it was exclusive. In five minutes, Dr. Prannoy Roy called to say: 'Wow, Sanjay. Great job today. How did you pull this off? And we can give SUN TV that footage.' I rang Kalanidhi back and told him that a tape could be picked up. Kala, as we call him, thanked me profusely. A media baron need not have called directly but I found him to be genuinely humble and gracious. It's not always that a national channel lends footage to a leading regional player. Truth be told, it's usually the other way around. This alone felt good.

Being on top of the rally coverage, in some measure, made up for the loss of the midnight arrest scoop. I went home with that 'you win some, you lose some' feeling. And continued to bask in the warmth of the appreciation shown by the top boss.

22

TOUGH COOKIES!

YARS BEFORE THE ADVENT of the Live OB Van and Flyaway Live Kits, spy cameras of the shape and size of buttons or pens, a hidden camera story on television literally meant just that: the normal big Beta Camera, with tapes the sizes of bricks, competing with early Motorola mobile phones, had to be hidden. A shoulder bag was customised with one side cut to accommodate the camera lens and a thin black film stitched to conceal it. The Correspondent would be wired with a concealed lapel microphone and a Radio Frequency remote transmitter. Back then in the late nineties, this equipment was considered 'sophisticated', with periodic reminders from the headquarters to 'be careful with the gear.'

When you are straight out of college, a hidden camera operation would be quite an adventure. Not all these sting ops would be successful. Some would come a cropper due to equipment failure, or street smart 'targets' who would sniff out something brewing, or aborted missions due to other 'breaking news'. The ones that materialised into stories are worth recalling.

The 'Biscuit Bandits', as they came to be called, were striking at will, thanks to gullible passengers who, despite awareness drives and warnings ad nauseam not to accept food, especially biscuits, from co-passengers, would still fall for the trap. The gangsters used to operate on trains passing through Kolkata. Their 'investment' was limited to buying tickets in AC Compartments. Lacing biscuits with sedatives, they would offer them to unsuspecting passengers who would fall asleep and wake up in hospitals 24 hours later, minus their suitcases. I came across a passenger who was too clever by half. Having heard of the modus operandi of these bandits, he flatly refused eatables from strangers and even carried his suitcase to the toilet. Alas, he left his water bottle behind. The outcome was predictable.

G. Thilakavathy, the Inspector General of Police (Railways), had busted one such biscuit bandit racket. A renowned Tamil writer, the high profile IPS Officer understood how the media worked. This was an engaging story in the public interest, but merely an interview with the top cop and pictures of the suspects would not suffice for a television story. Sound bites from the victims were a must.

The victims were recuperating at the Government General Hospital (GH). But getting them on camera was a challenge. The Government Hospital staff were usually allergic to media presence owing to adverse reports about the conditions inside. There were newspapers that ran series of investigative stories titled 'Inside GH'. The sight of journalists would trigger a call for the security to throw them out!

Obviously such resistance had to be overcome in our pursuit of the interview. In any case, as the victims were in-patients; we were going to mosaic their faces to protect their identity. We first did a recce minus the cameras and identified the ward. The next step involved smuggling the camera inside and recording a quick interview. It had to be like a commando operation: 'Enter, Shoot & Scoot'. I told my cameraperson that we could pose as visitors from a remote village who had landed up in the city looking for an injured relative. This meant buying simple cotton slacks and small towels (*thundu* in Tamil); one to throw over my shoulder and one to tie like a turban around the cameraperson's head. Wearing rubber slippers, chewing betel leaves and carrying a few bananas and a bottle of water, we sauntered in speaking Tamil with a Madurai dialect. The camera bag was in place with a few new undergarments placed on top.

The next hurdle was communicating with the victims. They were from North India and did not speak Tamil. Wouldn't 'villagers' from Southern Tamil Nadu speaking Hindi arouse suspicion? However, luck favours the prepared. By the time we got inside, the ward was almost empty. And the two victims seemed to have regained complete consciousness. In my broken Hindi, I managed to get a few quick sound bites.

'Did you not see all the warnings against accepting food from strangers?' I quizzed a man in his fifties.

'Ha, yes. But they looked like such decent people.'

I nodded, and wondered if criminals were meant to look menacing!

'In our society, is not polite to decline food offered by others,' the other victim, a bit younger, chipped in.

At the end of the day, 'traditions' – such as never refusing food from others – trump awareness campaigns.

The duo narrated how the gangsters even claimed to have had knowledge of palmistry and had read their palms on the train. One of the bandits even showed them a family album to befriend them further and exchanged phone numbers and addresses. Their state of shock had more to do with a 'how could such nice people do this to us?' feeling, more than the actual loss of all their belongings.

'What did they predict for you? Did they foretell that you would be poorer by the end of the journey?' I couldn't help asking the gullible souls as we made a quick getaway.

23

FORBIDDEN ENTRY

AT TWENTY-FIVE, STRAIGHT out of Law School and having learned the ropes in television journalism for a couple of years, a slightly brash, adventurous spirit is only natural. Indoctrinated with the zeal to get the story, whatever it takes, I have had my share of thrills and spills. When I look back, I cannot even imagine doing half of what I did back then!

Renowned industrialist Dr. A.C. Muthiah had become the President of the high profile Board of Control for Cricket in India (BCCI). Not a week passed without some action or controversy on the cricket front. At the fag end of the year 2000, the BCCI had imposed a ban on a few players: former Indian Skipper Mohamned Azharuddin, my childhood favourite, along with Ajay Sharma and Manoj Prabhakar. This was obviously a top headline. When the Delhi office confirmed that the BCCI Chief Dr. Muthiah was in Chennai, I was asked to 'drop everything and just get us his take.' Every ten minutes, the Input Desk kept buzzing for an update. The pressure was mounting with every call.

The distance between the CIT Colony Chennai Bureau and Dr. Muthiah's palatial bungalow in Kotturpuram, called 'Adyar Villa', was only about 4 kilometres or a 10-minute drive. The protocol to reach him was always through his Public Relations Manager, Jayakumar. As was the job description of any PR man, Jayakumar was adept at keeping the media away during 'inconvenient times' and being most gracious when coverage was welcome. The present interaction fell clearly in the former category. So the usual route of seeking Jayakumar's nod before approaching the BCCI Chief would have been an own goal, or to use cricket jargon, 'hit wicket'. I went straight to 'Adyar Villa' and asked the security guard at the gate if Dr. Muthiah was at home. The guard was evasive but I was able to convince him to let me inside. I reached the verandah. The front door was open. I rang the bell. No one came out. I quietly walked in, calling aloud 'Dr. Muthiah!' In a few seconds, I got a call from the then Bureau Chief Jennifer Arul.

'Sanjay, what are you doing in Dr. Muthiah's bedroom?'

'Eh. What do you mean, Jen?'

'I just got a call from his PR guy Jayakumar. He says 'Madam, your correspondent Sanjay Pinto has gone into the bedroom of my Chairman.'

I could only guess that there were either CCTVs remotely monitored by the Security guard or the man just alerted the PR Manager on the phone and the latter came up with the exaggerated version to evict me from the spot!

'Oh Gosh! Jen, I am standing in the drawing room. but I guess it is near the entrance of what looks like a bedroom.'

'Get out of there at once,' she shrieked, more in amusement than anger.

I obediently left the building but waited inside the compound. By this time, Vijay Grover of Zee News arrived, followed by a few other Tamil news channels. There is always strength in numbers and we stayed put inside the sprawling compound.

Dr. Muthiah himself drove in about half an hour later.

I immediately apologised for the intrusion.

'What intrusion?'

I narrated what had happened and he chuckled: 'Oh Jayakumar was just being protective! Don't worry. He was doing his job; you were doing yours!'

An impromptu press interaction ensued. I even got an exclusive tête-à-tête with him.

When I reached the Bureau, Jennifer and a few other colleagues were in splits on seeing me.

'Peeping Tom journalist, eh?'

I joined in the laughter and rushed to uplink the interview and email the transcription.

Lesson of the day: It's not only the media that can sensationalise events!

24

GOOGLY TO SIR GARY SOBERS

ONE OF NDTV'S ASSETS in the newsroom was the Sports Desk, with the likes of Gulu Ezekiel, Sonali Chander, Misha Grewal, and Anasuya Mathur. All of them were adept in their field. Misha was a squash champion; Sonali a keen golfer. This was one team that was on the ball and always reasonable with overworked bureaus. The endeavour was to fill their Sports bulletins with as many local stories and interviews as possible, saving fresh content for the 'Good Morning India' sports section. Bureau Correspondents were given due prominence, with adequate research back up and support from the Sports Desk. Filing a story or interview for Sports was always fulfilling. That I was a sports enthusiast helped.

Gulu was the Sports Editor of the channel. A veteran journalist and yes, the son of poet Nissim Ezekiel (whose poems like 'Ego Tripping' were part of my English syllabus in school) he was on back-slapping terms with most sportspersons, both national and international. Not surprisingly, he was the first to get wind of the arrival of any big names to Indian cities. For some reason, Chennai drew many big stars from different sports; whether it was for the Chennai Open Tennis or to the MRF Pace Foundation. With the top cricket administrators in the country, like industrialists A.C. Muthiah and N. Srinivasan, based in Chennai, the biggest sportspersons, present and retired, kept flocking to the city.

Carribean great Sir Garfield Sobers had come down to Chennai and was a guest of the then BCCI Chief A.C. Muthiah. An interview with the cricket legend was any journalist's dream scoop. At a time when the current crop of cricketers made mega bucks with corporate endorsements, apart from match fees, why should a veteran genius be left behind? Now that was an aspect that did not present itself to my attention when I approached the great man for an exclusive sit down interview.

'What's your total viewership?' he quizzed me.

I rattled off a figure in hundreds of millions, thinking that he was trying to size us up in terms of whether it would get the desired reach.

'Hmmm. How much will you pay me?'

I was dumbstruck. I realised that my hundred million answer had backfired!

'Sir Gary, I am not that high up in the pecking order just yet. May I check with my headquarters and get back to you?'

'Of course.'

I called Gulu from the car.

'Gulu, Gary Sobers wants to know how much we can pay him!'

'Oh! We don't pay for interviews. We don't have a budget for that. I can only authorize an honorarium for guests. That's a pittance: two thousand rupees!'

'Gosh! That would be an insult, Gulu. Let's ditch the interview.'

I'm not aware if any other channels paid for an interaction. But the next day there was a press conference with Sir Sobers. I landed up with all my questions. It was time to be street smart, I told myself. After instructing the cameraperson to keep a tight frame, without the channel microphones, I shot one question after another. Sir Sobers was at his eloquent best. I stayed back after the presser. After everyone had left, I placed a chair in front of the camera and recorded the same questions I had asked at the interaction. In television parlance, it's called 'questions to camera'. It was not an exclusive. I did not call it that. The answers were to the original questions. I merely played around with the format. In any case, this was what prime time anchors would sometimes do with the 'abetment' and 'connivance' of reporters on the ground! It's called a fake live or a 'sim sat' (simulated satellite). The viewers may have ended up thinking it was an exclusive interview, although it was not projected as that. What is sauce for a Delhi anchor should be sauce for a Chennai Correspondent!

25

CHENNAI HOSPITALITY

ONE OF THE GROUSES I used to have in television journalism was the Delhi-centric mindset of national channels. Where you worked from mattered more than your designation. Those sitting in the headquarters called the shots. Always. So even if you were Bureau Chief or Resident Editor, a relatively junior person at the Input Desk could broadly dictate your schedule for the day, at least in terms of live Outdoor Broadcasts. I often wondered if it was akin to a Sub Inspector at the Control Room of the Police Headquarters instructing a Superintendent of Police of a district! But that was the structure and nature of news operations.

Para-dropping the big shots from the headquarters to regional bureaus for important news events was another practice. I have always welcomed the presence of senior colleagues, as it served a twin purpose, of watching them in action from close quarters, as a learning experience and also giving them a ringside view of the constraints bureaus faced. At one level, a tinge of disappointment would also creep in, almost as if a big eagle had swooped down to take away our crumbs! But then, television is a team game and there is no room to sulk. To be fair, the seniors have always been more than considerate. And fun. Most journalists are foodies. The profession is such that you never know when you will have your next meal!

Some memories are unforgettable: Rajdeep Sardesai devouring crab masala with us, along with several helpings of steamed rice at Anjappar restaurant; of Sonia Singh eating a simple meal at Amma hotel, hardly a fancy place, with cats running under the table (!); of Barkha Dutt wanting to visit the Marina Beach and relishing roasted corn smeared with lime and later taking the Chennai Bureau out to Tapas Zaara; of our Sports Correspondent Nikhil Naz insisting on tasting rabbit fry at Ponnuswamy hotel; of Manika Raikwar hanging out with my family at Elliots Beach, followed by dinner at Crimson Chakra; and of Manoranjan Bharti from the Hindi channel, consuming masala dosa at Saravana Bhavan and looking quite shocked at the amount of fruit juice I was downing.

But the most frequent traveller down South was Sreenivasan Jain. 'Vasu' as he is called within NDTV, knew only a smattering of Tamil but he could interact with the most diehard Dravidian party worker as if he were the boy the next door. The trick was to mix a couple of Tamil words in an English sentence in an attempted colloquial accent. At an AIADMK rally, Vasu was trying to capture the pulse of the average party cadre and ferret out reasons for the sycophancy Ms. Jayalalithaa inspired.

'Why is this admiration, this craze about *Amma*?' he quizzed a small group.

'Yes, yes, *Amma* craze,' said one, attempting to answer in English.

It had a cascading effect, with the others loudly proclaiming, in unison, '*Amma* crazy, *Amma* crazy,' as an amused Vasu looked on.

That evening, in keeping with the Chennai tradition, we took Vasu out to dinner. Chettinad cuisine caught his fancy. So the venue was Karaikudi, quite close to the Chennai Bureau. The others dining could be seen whispering about the celebrity guest in the restaurant. Vasu had his fill of parottas and chicken gravy cooked with a thick paste of curry leaves. While he chose to skip dessert, none of us had any inkling of what was in store, post dinner.

As we walked out, a small group of Vasu's fans mustered the courage to introduce themselves. In a mood to pull Vasu's leg, I mentioned to them that he is crazy about Tamil film songs. Not a killjoy, he played along and nodded.

'Sir, what's your favourite Tamil film song?'

'Oh, all of them. Can you belt out one?'

'Yes, any song that you can dedicate to Mr. Sreenivasan Jain,' I added.

In seconds, we could hear a number from the Tamil hit film '12 B', composed by Harris Jayaraj. '*Oru punnagai poove, siru pookkalin theeve, nee ennai mattum kaadhal pannu...*'

It was catchy enough for our star newsman to tap his feet and make a feeble bid to hum along.

In the car, I translated the lyrics of that love song for Vasu. He froze initially! After all, the character singing was a young man! But soon laughed it off, the sport that he has always been, before burying his head in his Blackberry to rehash a script.

A few years later, Vasu was back in Chennai. This time I was on Paternity Leave. NDTV was one of the few organisations that believed in the concept of dads playing their part. I remember asking the HR department, if I would be entitled to thirty days, instead of fifteen, as I had been blessed with twins! Vasu dropped in at home for a sneak peek at my new born angels fast asleep in their cradles. That was a scoop of a different kind.

26

A 'CELL'-OUT!

MERCURIAL, CANDID AND EMOTIONAL, Vaiko is one politician who does not mince words or pull his punches. You could always bank on him for an explosive, or at the least, a juicy, sound bite. News stories that revolved around his speeches or interviews invariably made headlines. The MDMK Chief also maintained a good rapport with the media, emotional outbursts against some sections notwithstanding. To many journalists, New Year's Day was not complete without Vaiko's Press Meet followed by a biriyani feast at 'Thayagam', the party headquarters in Egmore. It used to be an annual ritual. The first of January would often be a lean news day, except if there was an accident at some midnight new year eve bash. It would not be difficult to cull out a newsworthy story from an interaction with Vaiko.

The firebrand leader, who started his party after his exit from the DMK, was the most vociferous supporter of the Sri Lankan

Tamil cause and the Liberation Tigers of Tamil Eelam (LTTE). At a public meeting in Thirumangalam, Madurai, he once thundered: 'Yesterday, I supported the LTTE. Even today I am supporting the LTTE. Tomorrow I will continue to support the LTTE.' This was when the draconian Prevention of Terrorism Act (POTA) was in force. The Jayalalithaa Government, which had taken a hard line against threats to law and order and expressions of support for terror outfits, was quick to crack the whip by invoking POTA. Chief Minister Ms. Jayalalithaa had quoted Vaiko's speech in a letter to the then Union Home Minister L.K. Advani. The Tamil Nadu Government decided to arrest Vaiko in July 2002, under Section 21 of POTA for addressing a meeting for the purpose of encouraging support to a terrorist organisation.

There were initial hiccups in getting an arrest warrant but when it came through, Vaiko was on his way back from Washington DC via Mumbai. Combative as ever, he refused to be cowed down by the news of his impending arrest. From his hotel room in Mumbai, he argued that the banned Tamil Tigers had to be involved in the resolution of the conflict, just like the PLO in Palestine or the rebels in Northern Ireland.

I was at the Chennai Airport to cover the arrest. The Madurai Superintendent of Police, Ayush Mani Tiwari, had reached the airport to make the arrest. A large crowd of MDMK workers and their leaders were shouting slogans hailing Vaiko. It was chaos. I pitied the passengers who had to catch flights that day. There was hardly room to stand at the arrival point. Ayush, who later became a good friend, seemed not too pleased by the huge media contingent. In many cases, party workers tend to play to the gallery at the sight of TV cameras and that makes matters worse for the cops struggling to control the crowd. I understood his predicament but I too had a job to do. In all fairness, no restrictions were put on our coverage. The arrest itself was peaceful. Full credit to Vaiko for ensuring that his arrest did not trigger violence.

As he got into a police van, he accused Ms. Jayalalithaa of presiding over a 'fascist regime'. The police convoy drove to Vellore where Vaiko was to be remanded. For 19 months, whenever there was a hearing in the trial, I travelled to the Vellore Central Jail to cover Vaiko. I had never seen a man so determined, unfazed, and energetic, despite his long incarceration. Vaiko's decision not to apply for bail hit the national headlines. The usual mix of stories on the trial were punctuated by what we call 'offbeat' reports on his prison life. Vaiko, I gathered, spent considerable time reading the Bible and other books, writing and playing volleyball. The close to three hour drive to Vellore from Chennai always meant that Vaiko would be the only story from me for the day. Of course, this translated into the routine live reports from outside the Vellore prison gates.

As the Lok Sabha elections drew closer, following an appeal from many political leaders, the belligerent MDMK Chief finally agreed to seek bail from the Special Court. It was the first week of February 2004. A little before 10 a.m., the Vellore Prison gates opened. Waving enthusiastically to his party cadre, Vaiko emerged from the prison after 577 days, as my friend and veteran journalist G.C. Shekhar quipped: 'physically weaker but politically stronger'. Bolstered by the chants of his supporters, Vaiko made it clear that he was starting his election campaign from these prison gates and repeated his choicest epithet for the AIADMK government: 'It is a fascist regime.' As we obviously could not stop midway, set up the OB Van and do live reports en route, (although the news desk did ask if it was possible!) I sent what is best under these circumstances – a pre-recorded report that would be valid for a few bulletins and agreed to send updates through phone-ins, as we followed the convoy. The drive from Vellore to Chennai usually takes about 3 hours. With chants of 'Puratchi Puyal' (Revolutionary Hurricane) by his supporters all through the journey, prompting Vaiko to stop for a bit every two or three kilometres, his convoy took almost 8 hours to reach the city.

About 2 years later, Tamil Nadu was due for Assembly polls. As with most alliances, there are always rumblings over seat sharing and allocation. That an emotional politician like Vaiko would not take a raw deal lying down, whether over the number of seats or 'unwinnable' ones from the alliance leader, in this case, DMK chief M. Karunanidhi, was common knowledge. But soon the haggling over seats for the MDMK reached breaking point when Vaiko was finally offered 22 seats, against his minimum demand of 23. There had been murmurs about switching sides, owing to this stalemate. But my jaw dropped when I received a call from Poes Garden, the residence of Ms. Jayalalithaa, that Vaiko was meeting her that afternoon. I made a dash to the residence. What I saw revived memories of my school History lessons on there being no permanent friends or foes in politics. Vaiko was standing right next to Ms. Jayalalithaa, who announced his entry into her coalition. Stifling questions on how the two leaders could come together after one of them jailing the other for 19 months not long ago, Ms. Jayalalithaa sternly asked the media not to live in the past but look to the future. Vaiko chipped in to say that it was 'the finest moment in Tamil Nadu's political history.' This was twelve years ago and those words still ring in my ears.

I went back to the bureau, and asked the Video Editor to pull out Vaiko's sound bites in 2002 at the Chennai Airport and 2004 at the Vellore Prison Gate, in which he called the AIADMK government a 'fascist regime'. This was a story that did not need much of a script as the sound bites spoke for themselves. I began my story with a split screen with the timelines and played the 'fascist' outburst followed by the 'finest moment' oration and labelled it 'Tamil Nadu's Turncoats'. Soon enough, there were memes on text messages about the cross over. Come to think of it dispassionately, Tamil Nadu always had its fair share of fence sitters and 'blow hot and cold' politics. But none was as glaring; or as interesting as Vaiko.

27

MY FIRST VOTE

YEARS AGO, MANY OF us television journalists made a plea to the Election Commission of India (EC) to allow us to cast our votes at the polling booths where we were on duty. In Chennai, this would either be at a school in Gopalapuram where Karunanidhi, Stalin, and the Marans cast their ballots, or at Stella Maris College where Ms. Jayalalithaa would vote. The logic was that if officers on election duty could cast postal ballots, why shouldn't 24x7 TV journalists on poll coverage be given a similar opportunity. After all, we would be tied down to a live outdoor broadcasting (OB) spot, often from 6 a.m. till about 9 p.m., well after the end of the polling deadline. The request was turned down. Those unaware of this background may find it strange to learn that the first vote I cast was as late as 2004. This was not inside but outside the polling booth. And not with an Electronic Voting Machine! The EC's rejection of the representation was a blessing in disguise; from Cupid.

As I began my live reportage on every bulletin on the 10 May 2004, what I saw at about 8 a.m. changed my life forever. A fair, tall, slim, beautiful girl (quite the description in those matrimonial ads) in a full-sleeved white kurta and jeans breezed past my OB spot. At 30, most of my friends and well-wishers had given up hopes of seeing me 'hitched'. There was something about the way she walked, that dignified gait, that had me hooked. I was so smitten that I walked up to her, said 'Hi', introduced myself and handed over my visiting card. She responded with a smile.

'Hi. I'm Vidya from Doordarshan.'

'Oh ok. Joined recently?'

'Yes.'

'Hey, I've given you my card. What's your number?' I quizzed her, handing over a pad and a pen. She wrote down her mobile number. In a few minutes, the leaders began to arrive and we both got back to work.

The same evening, I had to dash out to Hyderabad to help my counterparts Uma and T.S. Sudhir, who had an Assembly election in addition to the parliamentary poll. On the flight, images of Vidya walking past kept flashing across my mind.

I was back in Chennai on the 13 May. The next day there was a press conference at the DMK Headquarters in Anna Arivalayam. My cameraperson Edwin had coincidentally taken cut away shots of Vidya. 'Cut aways' are recorded for editing purposes to cover jump cuts. Like a close up of a journalist sitting at a press conference, a pad, pen, ring, hands and so on. This footage is plastered over portions like sound bites that are chosen and cut in between for brevity. As I noticed this footage being previewed in the newsroom, I walked up to have a closer look, secretly rewinding and playing these pictures, without causing any suspicion! I called Vidya that evening to casually ask her if she would like to have coffee.

'Not today. I have to go to the tailor.' Point noted. She didn't say 'No'!

On 16 May she called to chat and to subtly suggest an outing. I was in the middle of scripting a story.

'Sure, we can meet a little later this evening. How about ice cream at Freeze Zone? You can come to my office and we can go from here.'

Vidya arrived on time. I later learnt that she had gone to the parlour. Ahem! I quickly wrapped up my editing, and piece to camera on the office terrace and we headed to Freeze Zone. We hit it off so well that we decided to drive down to Coffee, a popular hangout, where we shared a vanilla milk shake. This too didn't suffice. The next stop was Sathyam Cinemas for the film *Something's Got to Give*. In true filmy style, it was raining after the movie. I dropped Vidya back. We texted each other that night in agreement that the company was better than the movie!

It took precisely 5 more days and another date on the 21 May 2004 at the Marina Beach for me to pop the question. The immediate response was a delightful 'me too'.

For almost a whole year, the Marina Beach was a convenient spot to catch up, equidistant as it was from the Doordarshan office and the NDTV Bureau. The rest is History and

Chemistry! The best part is that our courtship was bang opposite the Police Headquarters where many of my friends were stationed. And no one knew that I was in love till I announced it about a month before May 2005 when Vidya and I exchanged rings. Lest I forget: thank you Election Commission; this was one vote that counted.

28

LANKAN 'CUSTOMS'

OVER THE LAST FOURTEEN years, the only times I've switched off my mobile phone was on flights. It now seems to be part of my anatomy, attached to my ear, and charges by my pillow when I'm asleep, dreaming of life minus the buzzing contraption, but without it I feel lost and restless. Such is the addiction or perhaps just the nature of 24x7 television journalism in a happening, politically volatile State like Tamil Nadu that the first task before an overseas trip is activating my global roaming. The visa is secondary! A practice that came in more than handy when, a few months after my wedding, I was assigned to cover the 2005 Asia Cup in Sri Lanka.

If you work for NDTV, then following every little rule is an unwritten code. So while a counterpart from Star TV chose to travel as a tourist entitled to a visa on arrival, I went though the rigmarole of getting a work visa from the Sri Lankan Deputy High Commission, presided over by a media savvy

Sumit Nakandala. After all, the previous year's tournament was such a packed official assignment, with not just the match updates but also 24 sponsored exclusive interviews with Rahul Dravid, Shoaib Akhtar, Dean Jones and Bob Woolmer, that we hardly had enough time to gulp down a bowl of oats for breakfast let alone digging into Sri Lankan delicacies like string hoppers and chicken curry! Even as cameraman Alexander Edwin and I were halfway through a piping hot cup of Dilmah tea and some high cholesterol cookies, the diplomat ensured that the visa reached the cabin. And to further ease our passage to Lanka, Nakandala offered to fax a letter to the Airport authorities giving them a heads up of the arrival of an 'NDTV Media Crew'.

The Standard Operating Procedure for an 'out of nation' trip was the preparation of an itemized list of equipment to be carried: from the camera to tripod, tapes, lights, batteries, cables and mikes. The list would have to be inspected, signed and sealed by the Customs officials while leaving Chennai. Ditto on arrival in Colombo. And the process repeated on our return. The purpose was just to prove that we were bringing back company owned electronic equipment that we took out of the country for official work obviating 'duty' complications.

The check list in place, the interviews fixed, the gear packed and yes, not to forget the 'House of Fashion' shopping requests from colleagues! Courtesy a close friend Amaresh Pujari, Chief Immigration Officer, the 'NDTV Media Crew' was served roasted cashew nuts at the Immigration Lounge before our flight to Lankan hospitality, that we later realised was more than just a 'mandatory' anti-SARS chemical spray on all the passengers! Edwin knelt down to say a little prayer for a 'safe trip'; praying for divine help that we could most definitely do with in this journey to an unpredictable land.

Venkat, a cameraperson who had also been doubling up as a reporter ever since the debonair Harsha Subramaniam quit Star News to join CNBC, was on the same flight. And didn't fail to flaunt his 'no visa' street smartness! 'Why did you guys waste time getting a visa and all that?!' On flights to Colombo, the challenge for the cabin crew is to serve refreshments between the time the seatbelt sign is switched off and the landing! And of course, 'anointing' us with the disinfectant spray! Almost as soon as the Cabin Crew muttered: 'Welcome to Bandaranaike Airport', our 'star' journalist grabbed his bags in a manner that reminded me of my Primary School years at Don Bosco, when the bell would ring at 3:20 p.m. and everyone would make a Usain Bolt dash to the building gate, only to calm down the second they reach the playground or the car park!

I fished out my badge of honesty: the itemized list of equipment at the Customs Counter.

'What's this?' the burly officer in uniform with a disapproving glance, demanded to know, even as Venkat breezed past the green channel with triumphant mockery and his equipment all packed like a true blue tourist with 'nothing' to declare, except ridicule for our 'play by the rules' credo.

'An itemized list of what we are carrying,' I shot back in a matter-of-fact tone.

'Do you have a bank guarantee?'

'What's that for?'

'A bank guarantee for what you have brought into this country?'

'Did I bring in some dangerous weapons of mass destruction?' I wondered, with a perplexed look, as Edwin tried to intervene: 'Sir, we are journalists from India.'

'So what? Where's your bank guarantee, Mr. Journalist from India.'

The tone of his responses got my goat and so I insisted on seeing his superior officer, as I switched on my mobile and hurriedly typed a text message to Vidya, my wife: 'Reached darling. Call you when I check into the hotel.'

'Sudusinghe. Deputy Commissioner of Customs.' The name board was as big as the ego of the big boss inside! Or so I discovered a few seconds into my conversation with him.

'We are journalists from India, from NDTV, here to cover the Asia Cup,' I started, with my mobile phone beeping. It was a text reply from my wife. 'We are only carrying necessary equipment for…'

'If you want to use your phone, do it outside my room,' Sudusinghe scowled.

'Oh, ok Sorry. Just that we journalists are wired all the time!', I tried explaining, while putting it on silent mode.

'See, Sir, we have a valid visa, our papers are all in order. We are here for a legitimate purpose. We have an itemized list of gear that we are carrying. Why do you need a bank guarantee? We've been here before following the same procedure.' As I was making an attempt to convince the stubborn officer,

I noticed Sumit Nakandala's fax message pinned on the notice board! 'Look, your Deputy High Commissioner in Chennai has also intimated you of our arrival!'

Sudusinghe was far from convinced.

'You are from Tamil Nadu, right?'

'Yes.'

'What if you have brought this equipment for the LTTE? What is the guarantee that you will take it all back to Tamil Nadu?'

'Whaaaaaat?' I shot back, wondering if this man was nuts.

'We are carrying a camera and related stuff, not belt bombs! You are welcome to check everything. This is our company-owned equipment. If we don't take it back, we will have to pay for it!'

'Give me a bank guarantee or you don't leave this airport.'

'Bloody hell!' I muttered under my breath. 'So are you detaining us? Are you detaining Indian journalists?' I asked him, my voice growing louder, as I decided to work the phones.

My first call was to my IPS Officer friend, Amaresh Pujari.

'Guru! These blokes have detained us here at the Colombo Airport because they suspect we are carrying cameras for the LTTE!'

Amaresh passed on a number of an official from the Intelligence Bureau, whom I could contact for help.

I rang but no response. Mine would have been an unknown number, I figured.

Edwin, my cameraperson, began to panic. 'I'm the sole breadwinner in my family, Sanjay…'

'Relax Eddie! I'm not doing your annual assessment now!'

I dialled Shankar Jiwal, another cop friend, who was Zonal Director, Narcotics Control Bureau, South India, to ask for the latest number of Pujith Jayasundara, who was his counterpart in the Drug Control Board, last year, and whom I had interviewed for a story on new heroin smuggling routes in the region.

'Sanjay, Pujith is now DIG of Colombo. Call him immediately.'

I did. Pujith picked up! And promised to help.

We were getting restless. It was almost 2 hours since we had landed. Time for some lunch. But hey, it was about time we were 'released'!

A multi-pronged strategy, I felt was the best bet at this stage, I thought. So my next call was to my senior colleague Barkha Dutt, Managing Editor, NDTV.

'Hi Barkha. We are stranded here at the Colombo Airport. These guys want a bank guarantee for the equipment we are carrying to be convinced that we will take it back home.'

'Oh God! Shall I fax them an undertaking that you will bring the stuff back?'

'No, it won't help. They are insisting on this bank guarantee. I have just enough foreign currency for this trip for our daily food allowance, hotel bills, travel, and other sundry expenses. So I can't get it here too.'

'What if we transfer funds to you there? Or wait; let me speak to the MEA.'

Barkha's intervention worked like magic!

In ten minutes, Sudusinghe called for me. We were sitting outside. After all, mobile phones were not allowed in his hallowed precincts!

'Your Embassy is on the line,' he said almost grudgingly.

'Hello Mr. Pinto. We've spoken to them. You are free to carry on. Have a good stay here,' said a lady in a comforting voice.

'Thank you, Ma`am. This is such a relief!'

'Bye, Mr. Sudusinghe! Will you come to Chennai sometime?'

'No.'

'Not even to accompany your President? I thought I could catch up with you again, if I line up an interview with your visiting head of State on Indo-Lankan ties!' I added sarcastically.

Walking out of the airport felt like an achievement! Edwin made the sign of the cross and wondered if our driver would still be around with the placard bearing our names. My mind was elsewhere. Would we still be able to get string hoppers and chicken curry for brunch?!

29

MIDNIGHT TRANSACTION

CHENNAI PAST MIDNIGHT THROUGH the eyes of top cops; that's what I experienced a few times while accompanying some of my IPS officer friends – like Karuna Sagar and Mahesh Aggarwal – on their night rounds. As Deputy Commissioners of Police (DCPs), once a week, they would be in command of the entire night patrolling. Night duty in the software industry is called the 'graveyard shift'. In policing, it's worse, as there are no separate night shifts. Every night, on rotation, a DCP is put on night rounds. It begins at 11 p.m. and ends with a Daily Service Report (DSR) to the Commissioner at about 6:30 a.m. It doesn't end in the strict sense because the DCP only manages a short nap and is back to work by 11 a.m. That means four hours of sleep between two full working days with a nocturnal extension.

For a 24-hour-TV journalist, packing in such activities was not easy. But, as a former IPS aspirant, I was keen to do it. That my boss, Jennifer Arul, happened to be from a police family – she was the daughter-in-law of the late Inspector General Of Police F.V. Arul – helped, as there were allowances made and I was permitted to report for work a little late the next day. It wasn't really a party. Staying awake the whole night was tough, but it was worth the loss sleep. The experience often sparked a slew of interesting story ideas as I was able witness a lesser-known side of the city.

One of the things I observed was how watchmen in residential buildings and even ATMs operated at night.

Mahesh explained that it was advisable to give them stools instead of chairs to sit. A stool has no arm-rest and so the likelihood of their falling asleep was lower. But few followed the instruction. Cost-cutting and not security was the priority; most guards were elderly retired people provided at discounted rates by agencies.

Crimes at ATM kiosks were on the rise. The time was ripe for a reality check at these centres; on how safe you and your money are at night. It was night rounds – as a journalist.

For over three hours, from 1 a.m. in the morning till 4 a.m., we criss crossed the city.

At Adyar, we found a security guard wrapped up like an Egyptian mummy! A mosquito coil under his chair explained why. The presence of a TV crew with even the camera light switched on was not enough to interrupt his deep slumber.

Ditto at Alwarpet, Besant Nagar, T. Nagar, Parry's Corner, Mylapore; all the security guards were probably into their seventh dream.

At an ATM in Santhome, we found the security guard lying on the floor inside, snoring away to glory. My cameraperson put the microphone right next to his face to record what we call 'nat sounds'. There was no response even as he entered the ATM, for which he had to move the guard's leg. We decided to wake the guard up. The man was justifiably startled.

'Who are you?'

We identified ourselves.

'Why are you sleeping? Shouldn't you be awake to safeguard the money in this ATM and customers who come here to withdraw cash?' we asked.

'Sir, I have not gone home for the last two days. I'm doing continuous duty. The person who has to relieve me has not turned up and there is no replacement. How can I stay awake for 48 hours?'

I felt genuinely sorry for the guard. Unscrupulous agencies cut corners and exploit workers who are paid a small percentage of what is collected from the customers. Banks fail to conduct checks and think their responsibility ends with signing contracts with security agencies.

I returned to my office in C.I.T. Colony at about 4:30 a.m. armed with enough footage to hammer out a hard hitting story: 'The City Never Sleeps?' As the lift stopped at the third floor, there was action replay! The security guard at our own office was fast asleep!

Apparently he too had been saddled with 'double duty'.

A few bank officials who had got wind of our shoot, landed up at the office the next day in a bid to persuade us to drop the story. They were unwilling to move a finger to address the glaring breach in their security apparatus, but had the audacity to try and kill a genuine news report.

'Please, at least, don't mention the name of our bank.'

'Why? Do you want your customers to have a false sense of security?'

I looked at the TV in the newsroom. The story was on air. I stepped up the volume. The bank officials turned red in the face and walked out in a huff. The truth is hard to take; but it must be told.

30

WAVING RELIEF

A LITTLE PAST 8 A.M. on a Sunday morning, one day after Christmas 2004, I got a frantic call from Hemang Badani, a friend and Indian cricketer.

'Sanjay, did you feel anything da?'

'Feel what, Hemang?!'

'Oh man! Tremors. I felt it. A lot of people are out on the street.'

'Don't tell me. I didn't feel anything. Let me check and call you back.'

I could not call Hemang back and I'm sure he would have heard me on NDTV in a bit.

I was scheduled to travel to Kanchipuram for the questioning of the junior Shankaracharya Sri Vijayendra Saraswati in the Varadaraja Perumal temple manager muder case (both the Seers have been acquitted by the trial court and no appeal was filed). I immediately called my Input Desk in the Delhi Headquarters.

Ekta Kohli was on duty. 'Reports of an earthquake in Chennai, Ekta. Please flash it. I can do phonos (a live phone report) for now. An efficient but slightly hyper desk person, Ekta screamed: "Patch" Sanjay to the PCR (Production Control Room), breaking news, earthquake in Chennai...'

As I reported panic reactions from parts of Chennai, my fiance Vidya, who was a Correspondent with Doordarshan called to say that sea water had entered the Ashtalakshmi Temple and homes in Besant Nagar, near Elliots Beach. It seemed like a strange phenomenon during an earthquake. Vidya had informed her newsroom but they did not seem to take the news seriously and hung up. I did. To save time, I called the Output Desk (responsible for putting news on air) directly. Arijit, a young journalist was in his seat. I had to argue with him for a bit before he reluctantly put me on air to do 'a short 1 minute phono on your sea water entering homes or whatever...'.

I remember trying hard to convince the Input Desk that something big was brewing and that I should stay on in Chennai instead of travelling about 75 kilometres to Kanchipuram for a story that would have merely involved a few live reports. 'Who will bother about this questioning of the junior seer when there is an earthquake and perhaps something worse here?' My pleas were not accepted and I was forced to drive down to Kanchipuram with the OB van!

Soon enough the 'sea water entering homes or whatever' turned out to be the killer tsunami. I was the first to break the news, although the term tsunami was known about an hour later.

I had almost reached Kanchipuram when the Input Desk called. 'Sanjay, please get back to Chennai.' There was no time for 'I Told You So' and I played the obedient soldier on the firing line as Generals who had never fought a war were giving directions.

One of our cameramen, Srinivasa Rao who was rushed to the Marina Beach was almost washed away by the waves near the Tamil Nadu Forensic Science Laboratory as the waves smashed through the compound wall. Rao had a miraculous escape. The camera fell into the water; it had to be discarded as saline water had entered the parts inside.

On my way back to Chennai, another game of ping pong ensued. 'Sanjay, rush to Cuddalore. Reports of mounting death toll are coming in from there.' I turned around again and sped away to Cuddalore, via Puducherry, about 220 kilometres from Chennai.

By the time I had reached Cuddalore and took my position in front of the camera at the OB spot, all I could see were bodies piled up. It was a terrible sight: children were missing; parents were missing; homes were washed away. All in a few seconds. The fisher folk were inconsolable. The sea which they had all along worshipped had turned tormentor. People were running desperately, frightened and wailing and hoping that the body being carried into a school ground was not that of their loved one. Many were too shocked to even grieve.

Going by the scale of the disaster, I knew I was in for the long haul. I had not carried clothes as when I had left home, I was supposed to return the same night. I was wearing an orange and red checked half sleeved shirt and blue jeans. This is when the practice of having a small travel bag packed and ready came in handy. This was at home in Little Mount. More teams were being rustled up for the coverage. Supriya Sharma from the Mumbai Bureau had already landed in Chennai and was on the way to Nagapattinam, as was my senior colleague Barkha Dutt. I requested Supriya to have my bag picked up from home on her way from the airport. Covering such a massive tragedy can be emotionally very draining. I was exhausted but lost my appetite. My head office wanted a script for which I was too tired. Another senior colleague Sonia Singh for whom I have always had a lot of respect and affection, called to say: 'Sanjay, just dictate what you can; some case study. I will take it down here and have it voiced. We will use bits from your OBs as a Piece to Camera (PtoC) for your story.' I remembered what one of the kids had told me about playing cricket when the giant waves struck. More reinforcement, as it were, from my office arrived. This time, it was my counterpart from Bangalore, Maya Sharma.

Over the next few days, the Tamil Nadu Government, headed by Chief Minister J. Jayalalithaa left no stone unturned in their relief efforts, opening camps, temporary shelters, canteens, and it fielded some of its best bureaucrats to oversee the operations. Reports also came in of the Cuddalore Collector Gagandeep Singh Bedi rolling up his trousers and helping in evacuation to the point that he was almost swept away by the waves. Dr. J. Radhakrishnan, who had supervised the aftermath of the Kumbakonam fire accident in a school in which 94 parents lost their children, was rushed to Nagapattinam where almost the same number of children had lost their parents. Santha Sheela Nair, Vivek Harinarain, and a battery of senior IAS officers were camping in the two districts – Cuddalore and Nagapattinam – ravaged by the tsunami.

It was difficult to get accommodation in the few hotels in Cuddalore as many Ministers and their followers had also been sent to join in the relief and rescue efforts. The Government Public Relations Wing, however, stepped in to reserve a few rooms for the media. I managed to get one for my team. The next morning, as I headed out to meet survivors, I made a mistake in my reportage. I'm usually a sensitive person but I rather thoughtlessly asked a boy to tell me how it all happened, not realising that I may have rekindled those tragic images, even if it had been just 24 hours ago. I had hardly slept the previous night but that was no excuse. It's a lesson I will never forget, and one that was later raised at an interactive session at the Asian College of Journalism.

By the afternoon, I moved to another area in Cuddalore. It takes all kinds to make the world. There were curious onlookers who perhaps viewed the tragedy as an opportunity for disaster tourism. And there were those out to feather their nests with publicity. A small group of well-dressed people from a 'social service organisation' had landed with food packets. There were hungry children gathered there who were staring at the food. What was stopping these self styled 'social workers' from distributing these food packets to those devastated and hungry kids? Hold your breath. A few more press photographers who were on their way! I thought to myself; just like justice which must not merely be done, but should be seen to be done, relief work too, it seems, must be seen to be done. Tragedy may be a great leveller; but it is also a teacher.

31

MINISTER BACK TO SCHOOL

WHETHER YOU WERE A topper or mediocre, courteous or notorious, schools always take pride in inviting alumni who become successful in life. The more powerful you are, the warmer is the reception. Forty may have been the pass mark (35 initially) in school, but 40 in Tamil Nadu's Parliamentary election meant a centum. The DMK-led rainbow coalition had collared all the 40 seats, 39 in Tamil Nadu and the lone constituency in Puducherry. Jiving his way to the Congress-led Union Cabinet was Dayanidhi Maran, former co-owner of a Chennai discotheque Hell Freezes Over (HFO), son of veteran DMK leader Murasoli Maran, and grand nephew of M. Karunanidhi. Dayanidhi had just made his debut in politics, winning the Central Chennai Lok Sabha seat that, for long, had been occupied by his late father and former Union Minister Murasoli Maran.

'Daya', as he is called by his friends, was a high profile Minister of Communications & Information Technology. That his elder brother, Kalanidhi Maran, was a media baron, helped in projecting him as one of the prominent faces of the DMK in the national capital. A suave, English-speaking Minister, holding a plum portfolio, would naturally invite considerable media interest. NDTV's varied and exhaustive programme schedule which is called a Fixed Point Chart (FPC) lent itself to wide coverage of newsmakers. 'Youth Unplugged' was a popular show that placed young political leaders among school and college students for a freewheeling chat, with an anchor, of course.

I was assigned this show for two reasons. The DMK was part of my beat; and Daya had been my school senior at Don Bosco, Egmore. I reached out to him and got his nod for the programme. A show of this nature comes with a lot of leeway for creativity. I was toying with the idea of getting Daya to wear the Don Bosco school uniform of a white shirt and grey trousers. As the anchor, I would also turn up in the same attire. But, what should have been a foregone conclusion was headed for an anticlimax. The then Principal of the school, Father Rajashekhar Reddy was not too enthused with the idea.

'We have exams coming up and my boys will get distracted.'

'Father, it's only a half-an-hour shoot. And the guest and anchor are Past Pupils! The subject is a Minister, not a movie actor!'

That my mother, the late Mrs. Judith Pinto, had been a teacher of the school for over three decades, and that I had presided over many functions there as Chief Guest, did not, sadly, seem to count for anything.

'That is extraneous. Sorry. We want to improve our results. It will be a disturbance.'

Daya had kept his DB attire ready and had even fished out his old badge from the attic and could not believe his ears when I informed him that Don Bosco was not game.

Any school would have jumped at the opportunity. It was not just half-an-hour of prime air time on national television. Besides studying about our Parliamentary system in textbooks, here was a chance for the students to come face to face with their super senior who now walked the corridors of power.

Daya seemed dismayed by the Principal's intransigence and called to check on my Plan B.

'Sanjay, let's not force them. Please see if you can line up any other school in my constituency.'

This was Central Chennai and home to several schools.

I dialled another school Headmaster. This was a relatively low profile institution: MCC School on Harrington Road. The Headmaster Mr. Manohar found it hard to hide his excitement and almost literally rolled out the red carpet.

I must confess to being a trifle apprehensive about the confidence level of the students here. The show was designed to showcase the maturity, innocence, and general awareness of school kids, and give them a platform to rub shoulders with young politicians. I gently offered to coach the kids before the programme but the teachers assured me that I would not be let down.

Daya turned up well on time in his favourite sky blue shirt. The Assembly Hall was thrown open and a group of about thirty Class IX students were seated neatly in four rows. What followed had me and Daya stumped. The kids were in full flow and reminded me of the proverbial 'Ugly Duckling' transformed.

'What steps will you take to increase the tele-density in India?'

'How will BSNL compete with private mobile operators?'

'How will you sustain your 'Hello One Rupee and Kilo One Rupee'?[1]

'When will you abolish roaming charges?'

'Why is our internet penetration not high enough?'

'Sir, is it true that your primary mobile number is not a BSNL connection? If so, why not?'

Daya was in his element and seemed to relish his interaction with these exceptionally bright kids.

Towards the end, he chuckled: 'I don't face such challenging questions even in Parliament!'

What was on display was a 'middle class' school fighting to prove a point that they were in no way inferior to the clutch of elite institutions in the vicinity. Come to think of it, the boys

[1] This was a reference to the Minister's election slogan of mobile calls at One Rupee and Rice at the same price per kilogram.

of MCC more than lived up to Don Bosco's motto: 'Strength Through Hardship.'

As we wrapped up, I couldn't resist telling Daya: 'You will have your task cut out when these boys turn voters!'

32

UNEXPECTED 'BITE'!

ALWAYS IN THE NEWS for his wisecracks and political rhetoric in the capital, Mani Shankar Aiyar is a familiar face even to those down South. I was in Delhi in the mid-nineties to represent the Dr. Ambedkar Government Law College at the Mukherjee Memorial All India Inter-Collegiate Debate hosted by St. Stephen's College. The grand finale was an occasion for celebrity spotting. Mr. Aiyar was seated in the auditorium, a few rows away from my team. He was not wearing his political hat but was present in his capacity as a parent of St. Stephen's, where one of his daughters – Suranya Aiyar – was also an office bearer of the College Debating Society.

After the debate, Mr. Aiyar walked up to the Chennai teams and introduced himself. 'Hi. I'm Mani Uncle. As an MP from Tamil Nadu, I'd like to invite you over to my home for lunch tomorrow.' As students, we were taken aback by the invitation. MPs were not known to be this cordial. Mr. Aiyar's gracious wife and his daughters joined the three Chennai Debate teams for lunch at the lawn. I was bang in the middle of my preparation for the Civil Services Examination and so wanted a generic take on the career option from former diplomat. 'The Civil Services must be abolished,' Mr. Aiyar thundered, and suddenly broke into a chuckle, adding that 'it's not to dissuade you, my friend.'

A few years on, that view ought to have been of some consolation but strangely, it wasn't, as I didn't make the cut in that fiercely competitive test and had joined NDTV instead. Although I had kept in touch with 'Mani Uncle', through Deepavali and New Year wishes, I'm not sure if he really remembered me as the Law College boy he had invited home for lunch a few years previously, when my quest for a sound 'bite' took on a curious twist!

Hitting the campaign trail at the hustings may be an action packed and fun assignment. But it calls for a great deal of stamina. It's not just braving the peak summer heat and keeping pace with the convoys of the high profile contenders but also keeping the gastric juices in your stomach at bay. The unwritten code for a television journalist in the thick of election coverage is this: 'Stock up when you can. Don't complain when you are famished.' Hogging time is breakfast. That it's usually complimentary helps.

The NDTV style of election reportage involves following a big political leader for 24 hours. Not the entire period but pretty much from the time they wake up to the final rally for the night before the Election Commission deadline.

In April 2004, my cameraperson Arasu Arumugham, a real work horse who could slog 24 hours flat with hardly a break, accompanied me to Mayiladuthurai. My brief was to profile the Constituency. The effervescent Mani Shankar Aiyar was in the fray from Mayiladuthurai in Tamil Nadu in 2004. Having won twice in the past, the Indian Foreign Service officer and blue eyed boy of Rajiv Gandhi turned politician, projected himself as a son of the soil, the distinct *brahmin* accent notwithstanding.

Post breakfast, we headed out to shoot, focussing on drought, woes of farmers, and local issues; and the contenders, of course. Although it was customary for the political party units to give out pamphlets with the campaign schedule of the big guns, especially Ministers, we were able to spot Mr. Aiyar only around 3 o'clock. We were in one of the interior villages where no food was in sight. Not even a bunk shop selling bananas or biscuits or peanuts. It seemed like a *bandh* day. Arasu didn't mutter a word. But the hunger pangs were beginning to take a toll on me.

By the time we wrapped up the interview with Mr. Aiyar, it was close to 4 p.m. I could have fainted; Arasu too looked weary. As we were packing up, the local party officials invited us for a late lunch. Our usual refrain, 'Thanks, we've already eaten' came out spontaneously, but with deep seated regret! The man in charge either read our mind or saw the hunger in our eyes. 'That's ok. Sir specifically asked us to make sure that you have your lunch as there are no hotels in the vicinity.'

That's some pulse of the area, I thought to myself.

Reluctantly, Arasu and I gave in and went inside a tiled house, where we could see Mr. Aiyar sleeping soundly.

I whispered to Arasu. 'Even curd rice will taste like biriyani now.'

The banana leaves were laid out. What was placed on them shocked us: Prawn fry. Mutton biriyani. Eggs. Liver fry. Aiyar food was 'higher' grub!

The look on Arasu's face was a Kodak moment in a pre-selfie age!

I couldn't help wondering if the politician who is often accused of putting his foot in his mouth, had cultivated this hospitality during his years as a diplomat. Frankly, I don't think the lunch invitations, back in 1996 and in 2004, were even a Public Relations exercise. It was just courtesy. Period.

We were not diplomatic though. The sumptuous meal didn't colour our report which was suitably critical, dwelling on the need for better infrastructure in the village. I must admit though, that this was one story that I very nearly signed off with a burp!

33

WIT OF THE FATHER

THE RESULTS IN BY-ELECTIONS are usually a foregone conclusion. The party in power wins convincingly with huge margins. It's a stamp of authority in a sort of mid-term referendum. There are, of course, honourable exceptions like the R.K. Nagar by-poll in Chennai, to fill the vacancy created by the death of Late Chief Minister Ms. J. Jayalalithaa, which AIADMK breakaway leader T.T.V. Dhinakaran won in 2017 by a margin of over 40,000 votes, as an independent candidate against the might of the ruling dispensation. Unless it is a high stakes battle in which a Chief Ministerial candidate is in the fray or a high voltage contest with allegations and counter charges levelled by the rival parties inviting the attention of the Election Commission, the national media gives them just a mention on the ticker.

The death of veteran DMK leader P.T.R. Palanivel Rajan, former Speaker of the Tamil Nadu Assembly and sitting

Minister in the DMK Cabinet at the time of his demise in 2006, led to a by-poll in the Madurai Central assembly constituency. This seat was in the news following the Election Commission's decision to transfer police officials in the run up to voting. For decades, Madurai in Southern Tamil Nadu, remained the stronghold of DMK Chief Mr. Karunanidhi's elder son M.K. Azhagiri. Public perception was that Azhagiri's writ ran throughout Madurai. A by-poll here was obviously a matter of prestige for him to demonstrate his clout in the region.

The channel headquarters was quite intrigued by the Azhagiri factor in elections. I suggested an exclusive interview with him, which they immediately lapped up and sanctioned. After working the phones with Azhagiri's office and getting a confirmation of the interview, I flew down to Madurai and drove straight to his Sai Nagar residence, a landmark in the temple city. When I reached the area, my car was stopped by the police. We were frisked. I initially attributed it to the heightened security arrangements in place for the by poll. Little did I realise that a hundred metres away, Azhagiri, his son Dhayanidhi, and his supporters would be seated on cane chairs in one of the by-lanes under the trees. It seemed straight out of a film scene!

'*Vanakkam*. I'm Sanjay Pinto, NDTV.'

'*Vanakkam*. I have seen you on TV. Please come.'

Although I had taken sound bites from Azhagiri on many occasions in the past, this was my first one on one meeting with him. I must admit that he came across as quite suave, unlike the rough and tough image portrayed.

I cut to the chase.

'Law and order is not what it should be in Madurai.'

'Who says that?' he shot back in a tone that hinted at a little anger.

'That is the public perception.'

'Public will say a thousand things. It is fine here.'

'What about the Election Commission's view of Law and order in Madurai?'

'They have not said Law and order has broken down here.'

'But they have called for the transfer of police officials in Madurai,' I retorted.

Azhagiri smiled, took a deep breath and quipped: 'Thankfully, they have not asked for the voters to be transferred!'

I thought to myself, here's a man who has inherited the wit of his father. That sarcasm was headline material.

After quizzing him on the simmering intra-party and family tension, and local issues, in response to which he described a leader as a 'speck of dust', I wrapped up the tête-à-tête. By the time I reached the Madurai Airport, the interview was a headline. The satisfaction of seeing your work on air is unbeatable. The satisfaction of watching co-passengers discussing the utterances animatedly, then recognising you and seeking your perspective on all things political, was also something to carry home.

The DMK romped home in that by-poll with an impressive margin, polling more than twice that of its nearest rival from the AIADMK. Azhagiri had earned his smirk, and kept his prestige intact.

34

SUPERSTAR AS CO-PASSENGER

WHETHER IT IS POLITICAL leaders or film stars, access in Tamil Nadu, compared to many other States, is a different ball game. A cub reporter in Delhi or Mumbai may be able to almost effortlessly saunter into the offices of such personas. In Tamil Nadu, it takes years to break into the 'inner circle' to get through to the top bosses. Rajinikanth's larger than life cult status is attributable, among other factors, to his carefully rationed public appearances. Even for his own film releases, an exclusive interview is considered a scoop of the year. Frankly, the media needs the superstar more than he needs the coverage!

Rajinikanth was always a big name. But particularly after the release of his much hyped film 'Sivaji: The Boss', NDTV realised that stories on Rajinikanth translated into high Television Rating Points (TRPs). This meant the commissioning of special half-hour shows. In one of them, I actually dressed up like the superstar and did mimicry with some of his punchlines live on NDTV! Little did I imagine that I would end up performing what many discerning viewers labelled 'antics' by an otherwise 'serious journalist'. It was fun but deep down inside, I felt this dumbing down was not consistent with my image. But, just like marks to a student, TRPs mattered to a TV channel.

In keeping with this Rajini mania, NDTV decided to list the superstar as a nominee for its annual 'Indian of the Year' Award in the entertainment category in 2008. The Guest Desk called to ask me to give him 'a heads up' and based on votes from viewers, to get the elusive star's consent to fly down to Delhi to receive it. My first response was: 'This is mission impossible.' Here was an actor who hardly ever gave interviews to the media, save for a few sound bites to all channels in one go, granted just a *darshan* to millions of his fans before his film releases and often took off to the Himalayas to meditate after every project. How could I possibly make him commit to travel to Delhi and spend a whole day and night for NDTV? But Dr. Prannoy Roy insisted and you don't ever say 'No' to him. Not out of fear but due to his charm and the trust he places in you. 'Sanjay, if anyone can swing this, it's you,' he texted me. It was quite like an extract from a chapter of Dale Carnegie's bestseller 'How to Win Friends & Influence People'! The principle advocated was 'Give the dog a good name and he will go all out to live up to his reputation.' My reputation was on the line.

I knew Rajini's wife Latha, his daughters Soundarya and

Aishwarya, and also his son-in-law Dhanush, reasonably well. My first step was to send all of them messages about the award ceremony. Although the other nominees were big names like Shah Rukh Khan and Shilpa Shetty, I knew Rajini's fan clubs were hyperactive on social media and would be able to tilt the votes in his favour. Latha Rajinikanth called and got all the details, with Personal Assistant, and my namesake, Sanjay in the loop.

Unlike the headquarters, bureaus, except Mumbai, did not have the luxury of Guest Desks. So such tasks fell squarely on the shoulders of the Bureau Chief. But the News Desk would not accept just 'Rajinikanth Duty' as work for the day. To be fair, news could not be sacrificed. If there was a story, it had to be covered and the Rajini assignment, though high priority, had to always be in addition to the news of the day. For weeks, I was a persistent devil and kept calling and texting till Mrs. Latha Rajinikanth called me over for a chat over chilled buttermilk to the superstar's Poes Garden residence. I made a powerful pitch about the award ceremony and the high probability of Rajinikanth winning it. Dr. Prannoy Roy made a call to Mrs. Latha to bolster my efforts. That call was a turning point in making the superstar seriously consider the proposal.

In 2008, Prime Minister Dr. Manmohan Singh was also a contender for Indian of the Year in politics. As per protocol, an award could not be presented by one recipient to another. Although Dr. Singh was tipped to win in his category, an exception was made that if Rajinikanth were to emerge victorious, his award would be presented by the Prime Minister. This passed muster with Rajinikanth as it raised the profile of the event. Another visit to his residence, and another call from Dr. Roy, sealed the deal. What seemed like wishful thinking was suddenly catapulted to the realm of a schedule. The Travel Desk or Production Control took over the logistics and travel plans. But the tension till Rajinikanth actually boarded the flight was palpable.

I was obviously booked on the same flight but in Economy Class. Strategically, this was not a wise decision by the concerned team in Delhi. I could have easily swung a nice exclusive interview with the superstar on the flight. My role, I guess, was to just ensure that Rajinikanth was on that flight, and yes, to attend the event. In the world of copycat journalism, it does not matter if you don't do an exclusive, as long as the other channel does not get it! It was a late morning flight to Delhi, I checked-in and waited for the big arrival. Rajinikanth's staff were there at the airport to complete his check-in formalities. The Delhi office had invited the whole family and were hoping that one of his daughters, Soundarya, would also accompany him. However, only the star and his wife Latha arrived. A quick 'Hi' was exchanged.

Rajinikanth asked me again: 'Sanjay, the Prime Minister will be there?'

'Yes, of course,' I replied.

There was a mad scramble inside the airport for pictures and autographs. Rajinikanth obliged as many as possible and stood in the queue for the security check. However, the officers recognised him and frisked him quickly.

The Business–Economy Class disparity meant that I had

no further contact with Rajinikanth on the flight and even after landing at the Delhi airport. But my confirmation to the headquarters that Rajinikanth and Latha had boarded the flight was enough for them to take over.

We checked in to the Taj Palace, which was also the venue of the Awards Ceremony that night. As the hotel was swarmed by the Prime Minister's Special Protection Group (SPG), I had to get a Security Pass on production of my NDTV Identity Card. When the news spread that Rajinikanth was in Delhi, several colleagues requested me to organise photographs with him. But there was a strict ban on this practice imposed by the head office so that our VIP invitees were not disturbed. The only exception made was for my senior colleague Sreenivasan Jain, who was also a co-compere of the event. I met Vasu, as we call him, at the hotel that evening and took him up to Rajinikanth's room. We rang the bell and the man himself opened it, wearing his bath robe. Now unlike most stars, Rajinikanth has never been caught in an image trap. Off screen, there is no wig and no makeup. What you see in movies is very different from the man in person. Vasu kept looking around, till I nudged him. 'This is Mr.,Rajinikanth!'

I did the honours. 'This is Sreenivasan Jain, our Managing Editor,' I told Rajinikanth.

Vasu recovered quickly. 'Oh Hi! So good to see you in person.'

The conversation was brief as the superstar was just about to get ready.

I could have laughed my guts out on the way out but kept

a straight face, with great effort. Vasu got a call and said he would catch up later that evening.

Rajinikanth turned up at the banquet hall wearing a spotless white kurta pyjama, along with Latha dressed in a grand saree. Mrs. Radhika Roy instructed me to be by his side till the start of the function. I walked up to him and asked if he was comfortable.

'I feel at home, Sanjay. Thank you.'

In a few seconds, the then Union Finance Minister P. Chidambaram arrived and went straight to shake hands with Rajinikanth, exchanging pleasantries in Tamil. Mukesh Ambani was next and I could hear him greeting the superstar. Rajinikanth seemed a tad shy of all the attention. Almost on cue, the hall filled up with all the big stars. Karan Johar and Shah Rukh Khan walked in and wished Rajinikanth. I did not want to be seen as a spare part and went back to the NDTV staff row. Several colleagues complimented me for getting Rajinikanth to Delhi. 'What a scoop, what a big scoop!' was the refrain, although I kept wondering about the missed scoop in captivity, as it were!

Dr. Manmohan Singh's arrival marked the start of the event. The cameras kept focussing on Rajinikanth, making it seem that he was the de facto Chief Guest. When the NDTV Indian of the Year in the Entertainment Category was announced, the cameras panned to Shah Rukh, and Karan Johar seated beside him. It was Rajinikanth who went up on stage to receive the award. And yes, from the Prime Minister. I took a deep breath.

My promise to him was fulfilled. Now I could retire, at least for the day.

Vasu did the interview with him on stage. Rajinikanth did not hide his happiness on receiving the award from what he called the 'golden hands' of the Prime Minister, whom he referred to as a 'Political Saint'. The questions revolved around his possible and long-pending foray into politics and the usual diplomatic replies like 'if God wants me to enter politics, I will.'

Even as the event was being beamed live, I was flooded with messages from Rajinikanth's army of fans, thanking me and NDTV for the award. If a single story on the superstar would make our TRPs zoom, imagine the impact of that evening.

Questions were thrown open to the audience with Karan Johar given the first prompt. Pat came a *cliché*, at least down South. 'Is there anything Rajini can't do?' The guffaws indicated that it came across as original. Shah Rukh stood up with a wry smile and fired a salvo. 'Sir, what does it take to become a Shahenshah?' Rajinikanth shot back: 'Shah Rukh, don't worry, one day you will become a Shahenshah.' As Rajinikanth has always referred to Amitabh Bachchan as the 'Shahenshah of Cinema', I could not help wondering if this was a witty dig by Shah Rukh, known to have a way with words, and who is himself hailed as the 'Badshah of Bollywood'. Neither was I sure if the wit, if intended, was appreciated by the audience. Or if Rajinikanth took the exchange in his stride. The best way to find out was to call him. That night, I called his room and clarified if all was well.

'Sanjay, NDTV is happy, right?'

'Yes, Sir. Thrilled that you were there.'

'Then I am also happy. God bless you.'

What the Delhi office missed on the flight, they wanted to make up for, after the event. I was assigned the task of getting a sit-down interview with Rajinikanth for Sreenivasan Jain's show. The plan was to show up at the hotel room early morning and seek that interview. As Rajinikanth was known to be an early riser, I rang his bell at 7 a.m. Guess what, the superstar had left the hotel at 5 a.m. for the Himalayas!

God has his ways. For months on end, I regretted not persuading Delhi to send me business class and thus missing an interview on the flight.

It was two years later.

I was heading NDTV Hindu editorially as its Executive Editor–English News. Rajinikanth's next upcoming blockbuster was *Enthiran*, produced by Kalanidhi Maran. I got a call from Director Shankar's office to play a cameo in the film. My role was limited to an anchor link sitting in my news studio. The lines were predictable. 'Robot has captured ARD. Let's go across to our Correspondent on ground zero for a live account of what's happening there.'

Rajinikanth was to switch on the TV to see the news I was breaking.

When the movie released, a gang from the NDTV Hindu office went to watch it and almost brought the roof down when I appeared for all of 15 seconds. Come to think of it, that's the normal duration of a sound bite or a Piece to Camera in a news story. So we valued every second.

What I missed as a co-passenger, God gave me as a co-star: Rajinikanth. And of Aiswarya Rai Bachchan. Ahem.

35

MARATHON WITH THE CM'S DAUGHTER

THE FIRST TIME I had heard of Kanimozhi, it was in the context of a Karunanidhi family member working for *The Hindu* newspaper. Soft spoken but articulate, unassuming and affable, she had co-founded an opinion portal 'Karuthu' with Karti P. Chidamabaram to promote free speech. That was when I briefly interacted with her and got a short sound bite for a news story.

Although 'Kani', as she is called by her friends and family, was not too keen on politics, preferring her literary pursuits instead, the media kept a close watch in anticipation of her political plunge. I remember her father and the then Chief Minister Karunanidhi quibbling with words at a press conference at the Secretariat when asked if Kanimozhi would be nominated to the Rajya Sabha.

'*Yaar Mozhi Kani ah irukko, avangalukku vaippu kedaikum*,' (The person whose language is sweet, may get a chance). The DMK patriarch would always answer in riddles but I had back then interpreted this one liner as a confirmation of daughter dear's political foray. When that nomination came through, a newspaper headline screamed: 'Jaya, Here I Come', a reference to the DMK's new woman leader to take on the then AIADMK supremo Ms. J. Jayalalithaa.

Soon enough, Kani became literally the 'girl next door' when her family shifted from Oliver Road to a sprawling bungalow in C.I.T. Colony, diagonally opposite the NDTV Bureau. Outspoken and always accessible, Kanimozhi was the first choice for a DMK voice on any story or show. That she was our neighbour and would walk down to the studio made matters easier. I would often walked down with her and see her off at her gate, conversing in my slightly anglicized Tamil. Over time, Kani started referring to me as 'Pulavar Pinto', meaning 'scholar Pinto'!

The political avatar aside, Kani never gave up her literary and cultural interests and spearheaded a mega extravaganza, called 'Chennai Sangamam', to showcase folk art. Her partner in this exercise, Catholic Priest Father Jegath Gaspar, who was heading an outfit named 'Tamil Maiyam', went all out to make it a signature event in Chennai. Erudite and widely travelled, Father Gaspar once told me that he wanted to make 'Chennai Sangamam' like the Paris White Night festival.

The event was a hit, abounding in folk artistes performing to ecstatic crowds and food stalls selling mouth-watering dishes from the South like Dindigul Venu Biriyani, Tirunelveli halwa and Jigarthanda. There were sponsors galore, with real estate firm 'Marg' coming on board as the title sponsor of the 'Give Life' Chennai Marathon. NDTV loved colour stories, especially ones that showed politicians in the thick of them. There was a share of controversy too with questions raised over why the State Government was seen to be backing a private endeavour.

If the Mumbai Marathon got television channels excited enough to dip in and out of bulletins with live coverage, the Chennai event was not to be left behind. Live reports were planned from six in the morning. An event of this nature would require several pre-recorded reports as the OB Van would take at least fifteen minutes to set up at different points along the route.

Kanimozhi was the main organiser. After my pre-recorded interview with her, I jocularly suggested:

'Kani, you are in your tracks and keds. Why don't we do a chat while running, say 100 metres?'

Frankly, I expected her to politely decline. But I was taken aback when she shot back:

'Ok. But can you run too?'

Being on the heavier side, I guess my school athletic past was far from evident!

We began to jog: Kani seemed much fitter and I was the one struggling to catch my breath.

The anchor in the studio, Gargi Rawat, looked both amused and impressed and commented after the interview: 'Kanimozhi quite the sport there.'

That she certainly has been, in the years ahead, facing all the challenges, including imprisonment in the 2G case, head on and emerging stronger. The race is on; the baton will pass on to her some day.

36

HEAT OF THE MOMENT!

THE EARLY BIRD SELDOM gets the interview; it's usually the better connected one which does. And if it's Doon School in the North, Don Bosco is the coveted South Block where contacts are made for life and nurtured. The crème de la crème send their children to this Salesian-run school in Chennai's upmarket Egmore area. To a child from a middle class family, this would have been the most unlikely destination. But when your mother teaches in this school and your father is determined to give you the best education, exceptions are made.

My mother, better known as 'Judy Pinto Miss' in school, was Karti Chidambaram's first teacher. P. Chidambaram was then a leading lawyer of the Madras High Court and a Congressman. By the time his only child Karti became the School Pupil Leader, narrowly defeating Arvind Pandian, the son of the Tamil Nadu Assembly Speaker P.H. Pandian (who had propounded the Speaker's Sky High Powers doctrine) in the election, Chidambaram was the Minister of State for Home. The Chidambaram family was very attached to the school, with Karti's mother Nalini, also a lawyer, even sponsoring the education of several poor students. As I was 3 years junior to the VIP brat pack, I hardly got to interact with Karti, who, like his father, was a tennis player and didn't have much time to play crocker with the rest of us. This was a game almost patented by DB: half cricket, half baseball and half out! But we knew each other and kept in touch. There were many more occasions to interact after I entered the media and he, predictably, took the political plunge.

P. Chidambaram is undoubtedly an extremely intelligent and suave politician but you can get easily snubbed by him! I've covered his campaign from Sivaganga over four Lok Sabha elections. By 2004, Karti had emerged as his father's own Home Minister, camping extensively in the constituency and bolstering the campaign with his inherited oratorical skill that applied to chaste Tamil as well!

Getting an exclusive interview with a national figure like P. Chidambaram, not just at election time but also during the debate on the OBC reservation quota, was every journalist's goal. I called Karti to intercede on my behalf. The father-son rapport was great and it clicked.

'4 o'clock at home. Come there and set up a little earlier.' Karti's call lifted my drooping spirit at a time when such scoops were hard to come by.

'Thanks Karti; will be there! Are you also going to be around?'

'No, I'm in Sivaganga. But my father's Media Secretary Thirunavakarasu will be there to help you. He will call you to coordinate.'

The Chidambarams live in a bungalow on the posh Haddows Road.

I got there at 3 o'clock with a two-camera setup along with camerapersons Sagayaraj and Arasu.

Thirunavakarasu was waiting for us and directed us to a room where the interview was to take place. As the camerapersons were setting up the lights and zeroing in on the best backdrop, Dr. Srinidhi, Karti's wife walked in to greet us, with her daughter Aditi.

We chatted for a bit and waited for PC to arrive.

At five minutes to four, his convoy drove in.

Clad in his spotless white, crisp shirt and *veshti*, he looked tired but his face brightened as soon as he saw his granddaughter playing near the staircase with a small cart of toys. PC looked every inch a doting grandfather.

I butted in. 'Good evening Sir. I'm ready for the interview.'

'Good evening. Please give me a few minutes to freshen up.'

PC walked in looking all set, took his seat and was pinning the lapel mike.

'This place is so warm. Why did you fix it in this room? There is no AC here.'

I had no answer as the spot had been picked by his Man Friday.

PC looked perturbed. The room was slowly turning into a mini furnace with the 1000 watt bulbs that our crew had switched on, making it worse. Sweat beads started appearing on his forehead.

'I'm not doing this interview here,' PC snapped, glared at Thirunavakarasu, and began to storm out.

'Sir, sir, mike,' my cameraperson feebly reminded him.

Thirunavakarasu followed PC trying to explain why he had chosen that room.

'See, I have to wash my face again.'

My mobile phone beeped. A text message appeared on the screen. 'ETA of your Chids intw?'

'Didn't happen; will explain soon,' I texted back.

I called Karti and told him about what had happened.

'Must be a communication gap. Let me get back to you.'

Later that evening, Karti called back.

'Is 8 in the morning ok for you?'

'Yes, sure but not in the same room!'

'Don't worry. It will be worked out.'

This time, I didn't inform my office about my second attempt. If it happens, let it be a bonus, I thought.

We arrived at 7:30 a.m. Thirunavakarasu was waiting and ushered us into a really cool glass room overlooking the garden. The AC was already running. It reminded me of how the drivers of many political leaders turn on the car ACs at least fifteen minutes before the VIP steps in!

PC was there bang on time. Even before I could explain how it just wasn't my fault yesterday, he smiled and said, 'Sorry about the mix up yesterday.'

I was relieved. PC was in a very good mood and what was meant to be a short five minute chat went on for twenty two minutes: enough for a full length 'Talking Heads' show.

'I'm glad you walked away yesterday, sir!' I couldn't resist telling him. 'Thank you!'

'Thank your school mate,' he said and left to meet a group of party workers who had gathered at his residence.

The patient bird also gets the interview; and a longer one at that!

37

POLITICIAN TO COURT

IT WAS CLOSE TO the last leg of my stint as Bureau Chief with the national channel, NDTV 24x7. Part of my duties included roping in the 'biggies' for prime time shows. Dr. Anbumani Ramadoss, who was then the Union Health Minister, had come to the studio for a debate on the Ban on Smoking in Public Places which kicked in around Gandhi Jayanthi. After the show, as I saw him off to his car, he asked me 'So Sanjay, do you exercise?'.

'Not regularly, Anbu. Where's the time? See it's past 10:30 p.m. and I'm still in office. We do play badminton occasionally.'

'Oh! You play baddy. Where?'

'We are like nomads and go wherever we manage to gain entry into a good court! So far, at the Alumni Club, courtesy a colleague, Upendaran, who is a member there; at the Presidency Club, thanks to my friend Priya; and sometimes at the IPS

Mess with my officer friends. You see, there such a shortage of badminton courts in Chennai.'

'Want to play with me sometime?'

'Sure!' I thought to myself, 'I can easily trounce him! He looks quite burly,' and wondered just how he would move around the court. 'Anbu, just name the place and date and time and I'll show up.'

'Ok, Sanjay. Any weekend between 5 and 7 p.m. at the Race Club. Call me or my PA Swaminathan to confirm. Good Night.'

As Anbu's car zoomed away, I turned to my cameraperson Edwin. 'Eddie, will he be able to return my smashes?'

Eddie too seemed excited as he was aware of his impending conscription to the game. He was quick to flatter: 'Even Gopichand cannot take your smashes, Sanjay!'

'You mean Gopi Chander and not Pullela Gopichand, right', I chuckled. Gopi Chander was one of our technical staff members.

Over the next few months, the breaking news rigmarole kept us on our toes with little time to take on the challenge thrown by Ramadoss.

The news cycle can be unrelenting. I had almost forgotten about this match.

Then came my deputation with NDTV Hindu as the Executive Editor. It was quite like captaining a Ranji Trophy side. I had the freedom to choose my team, play up stories as headlines on seventeen news bulletins every day, assign reports and do my own shows, one of them being a free-wheeling chat with political leaders and bureaucrats that I named 'Corridors Of Power'. A little before the Christmas season, I was able to sneak in some free time to unwind. In the media, you often tend to mix work with 'holidaying'. The symbol of the PMK party is the mango. And I hit upon the idea of downing two mangoes with one stone! Playing badminton and recording an episode of 'Corridors Of Power' with Anbumani at the court itself. I pitched the idea to Anbu and he seemed willing to take on my smashes and my questions in that order. The match was fixed! I preferred a doubles match as it afforded leeway to shift the blame, just in case!

With a headband, wrist band, a navy blue track suit, a red NDTV T-shirt and Yonex shoes, I made a grand entry into the Race Club Court. Anbu had not arrived, so Edwin and I did some stretching and hit a few shots to warm up. In about 5 minutes, the Minister walked in wearing a sky blue T-shirt and shorts.

'Hi Sanjay. Give me 5 minutes.'

What I witnessed next gave me the jitters. The man seemed super fit and his technique was flawless. And this was just his warm-up rally.

It took precisely 10 minutes for the match to be over. 21-0. That's right: twenty-one – love; we couldn't score a single point against him. What about my smashes? The shuttle landed like a mosquito on his racquet! What about his movement on the court? There was no need for that as we were the ones breathlessly scurrying from one end to the other as Anbu almost stood in one place and remote controlled us with sheer placement.

What I lost with the racquet, I more than made up with the microphone. From whether his party, which started off as a Vaniyar Sangam, blocking roads with felled trees, had decided to atone for its environmental sins with 'Pasumai Thayagam', a green initiative, and on to caste clashes and violence; from the denial of a Rajya Sabha seat despite DMK Chief M. Karunanidhi's comment on having 'Anbu (affection) for Anbumani' to dynastic politics and the party being a fence sitter; from his battle against the tobacco lobby to accusations about Malayalees 'dominating Central Govt posts', I 'served' quite a few volleys. Anbu was unfazed throughout the interview. As soon as I wrapped up the show, he ordered chicken sandwiches for us and sat down to have water melon juice. The conversation veered back to the ban on smoking. 'It's time people kicked the butt,' he said with a glint in his eye. I shot back: 'Anbu, that's what happened on court today!'

38

EXPLOSIVE INTERVIEW

ONE OF MY GRIEVANCES in television journalism was that when it mattered, like election time, senior colleagues would swoop down like eagles from the headquarters, collar the cream of our coverage and leave behind the crumbs for lesser mortals in the State bureaus. Sreenivasan Jain (Vasu as we affectionately call him) was an exception. As one of the Managing Editors of NDTV 24x7, he always upheld the principle of 'federalism', as it were, maintaining cordial Headquarter-Bureau relations. Adding value to coverage by dint of wider experience and exposure without stepping on the toes of the regional satraps or Bureau Chiefs is like walking a tight rope.

It was the run up to the 2009 Lok Sabha Poll. Having made a clean sweep in 2004, the Democratic Progressive Alliance (DPA) led by the ruling DMK was perhaps hoping for an encore. The Sri Lankan Army was waging what turned out to be the last leg of its war against the Tamil Tigers.

Whipping up Tamil sentiments was a predictable strategy by most parties here.

Almost every news channels was vying for exclusive interviews with the two Dravidian juggernauts: DMK supremo and the then Tamil Nadu Chief Minister M. Karunanidhi, and AIADMK Chief Ms. J. Jayalalithaa. Just like the Jesus through Mary route, the best person to intercede on our behalf with Karunanidhi was his pet daughter Kanimozhi. The media savvy Rajya Sabha MP, poet, and former journalist with *The Hindu*, was on good terms with most of us and would readily oblige whenever requests were made for a sound bite or a studio appearance for a prime time show on her party line. As the NDTV Bureau was hardly a cricket pitch away from her C.I.T. Colony residence, Kani (as she is addressed by many in the media) would often walk down to our studio without any security or even a PA. As a sign of courtesy, I would also walk back with her to her gate, chatting off the record, about political issues. Our request for a one on one with her father was on the table. When it was confirmed, Vasu flew down to Chennai. As Karunanidhi speaks only in Tamil, anyone else would have asked the Bureau Chief to play interpreter, out of the frame! Not Vasu. 'Sanj' (as he calls me) 'come along, let's do a joint interview.' Having covered the party and the political scene in Tamil Nadu for more than a decade, I was more than ready for an extempore interview, without the customary writing pad on the lap.

The paraphernalia that comes with a senior colleague from the headquarters is always an advantage. When we reached

Karunanidhi's house that morning, I took off my shoes at the door (a South Indian tradition) but Vasu chose to have them on. (Incidentally, the same pair that Bollywood actor Vidya Balan said she liked in a Bombay Talkies show!) I greeted the CM with a bouquet which surprised Vasu a bit. One of the rooms was converted into a mini Production Control Unit!

Karunanidhi was flanked by his Transport Minister K. Ponmudi, his wife Rajathi Ammal, Kanimozhi, and of course, his Secretary and shadow, Shanmughanathan. There were four seats in the room, two opposite each other, indicating that Kanimozhi was going to join the interview. Having studied in the Dr. Ambedkar Govt. Law College in Chennai and with the experience of covering the DMK for years on end, my spoken Tamil was good enough to interview 'Kalaignar' Karunanidhi. I often jocularly quibble '*Yaen Tamil yenukku perumai, mathavaluku poramai*!' (My Tamil is a matter of pride for me and jealousy for others). As Karunandhi took his seat, Vasu was powdering his nose. Trust the witty political leader to have his say. 'I'm the one giving the interview and you are putting on makeup!' Vasu retorted: 'You are so handsome that you don't need any!' A beaming Karunanidhi promised to answer questions in English at the next interview.

Vasu opened the interview with questions on the DMK's prospects and the Eelam card being played by parties. Although Karunanidhi understood most of the posers in English, Kanimozhi was translating them for him. When my turn came, I asked the DMK patriarch: 'In the present scenario, do you support or oppose the LTTE?' It was a loaded question. But I was aware that you cannot get a word to slip out of the mouth of a shrewd politician like Karunanidhi that he doesn't want to reveal. He dropped a bombshell. 'Prabhakaran is my good friend.' Chuckling, he added, 'And I'm not a terrorist.' Vasu was taken aback. The DMK was in an alliance with the Congress, whose late leader Rajiv Gandhi had been assassinated by the LTTE. The remark had the potential to snowball into a political controversy. The interview went on for another half an hour. I could sense a slightly uneasy expression on Kanimozhi's face, who also seemed surprised by the comment.

After the interview, Karunanidhi drove to the Secretariat. Shanmughanathan requested me to inform him about the airing slots. Rajathi Ammal served us chilled butter milk in the drawing room. Quite pleased with the cracker of an interview, Vasu began chatting. 'So what's the favourite dish you cook for Kani?' Rajathi Ammal smiled and said: 'Fish curry.'

Realising that the Prabhakaran comment could land the party in soup, Kani quizzed me: 'So Vasu is going to play up that bit is it? I swung this interview and see....' That remark was too juicy a headline to let go off. For the next 2 days, it was a top story on our channel and all the newspapers both in India and even some abroad. A senior journalist S. Murari texted me: 'Hey congrats! good interview. The delicious irony was that you were doing live analysis of that remark right outside his house.'

Fortunately for the DMK, the Congress spokesperson took the stance that it was Karunanidhi's personal opinion and the alliance was not affected. Being a former journalist herself,

I guess Kani understood the dynamics of the newsroom. It's a different matter that the next day, Karunanidhi conducted a mini press conference for the other English TV channels claiming that his remark was quoted out of context. The controversial bit was not spliced or edited but aired the way it was shot. And the camera never lies. We just reported the truth. There was an uneasy calm in the next few days but, at an impromptu fast that Karunanidhi undertook at the Marina to urge the Centre to protect Tamils in the island nation, I met Kani who came across as her usual cheerful self. There can be no permanent grudges in political reporting.

While the questions and answers in that interview may eventually fade away from my memory, I am unlikely to forget the spectacle of Vasu sitting cross-legged with a makeup kit on his lap and a mirror in his hand, hardly a few inches from the grand old man of Tamil Nadu politics.

39

'ROWING' REPORTER!

FLOODS EVERY TEN YEARS in Chennai: there had been a pattern to the monsoon fury from the mid-eighties. Staying close to the banks of the river as I did, I vividly remember vacating our tiny home in Little Mount to move into a neighbour's residence on a slightly higher level, in the winter of 1985. I guess my first candlelight birthday dinner was a little before I entered my teens! No power in the area, and all our valuables – TV, stereo, certificates, books – stacked on stools above a showcase, just in case the water entered our home. Action replay during the monsoon of 1995. Only this time we didn't have to move out, as water from the Chembarambakkam lake wasn't released and the level at the Marmalong bridge was just under control.

A hat trick in 2005! The difference this year was that I was a journalist, whose duty was not just to watch for the rising water level in the vicinity but to tell the nation about the havoc across the State, to tell them by showing them real visuals. The cliché – 'when it rains, it pours' – was playing out to the hilt. I still remember the date: Wednesday, 26 October 2005. My half-charged phone kept ringing as if it were on steroids! The headquarters had got wind of a storm brewing and a disaster in the making. The problem with TV channels is that they often have Generals at the desk who have never fought a war!

'All schools closed; power supply cut; trees falling; roads cut off. Sanjay, when can you do OBs for us? Can we have you live at 9?'

What colleagues, who are sitting paper dry in front of computers, far away North of the Vindhyas sometimes forget, in their zeal to get the best on air, is that if roads are cut off due to water logging and fallen trees, the situation would apply to those who are supposed to do OBs as well! And OB vans are not quite submarines!

It was hardly 5 months into my marriage. Vidya, my wife was worried. Justifiably; I was on medical leave, suffering from high fever. How would her hubby venture out in this torrential downpour? It turned out to be the maximum rainfall Chennai had experienced in a hundred years! 21 centimetres in just 2 hours. If you're a journalist, you just need to be out there, where it mattered; whatever it takes. I gobbled up some breakfast, popped a paracetamol tablet and got into my rain gear, which included rubber boots to wade through waist and sometimes even neck deep water with electricity flowing through! Thank God for small mercies. My Gypsy started with a single crank and as the engine roared, I set out waving to Vidya with a 'Don't know when I will return;

stay safe inside.' Pity, you can't practise what you preach in such situations.

I moved only in second gear, through water that almost touched my headlights. The Gypsy has a ground clearance of 210 mm, much higher than most other vehicles. Five minutes after I left home, my wipers gave up. But that was the least of my concerns. The only goal was to reach the office in C.I.T. Colony, Mylapore, and go out with my crew. Miraculously, I got there after many diversions along the way. My cameraperson Rajesh Swamy was also there waiting for me. Not wanting to get stuck somewhere, we decided to walk and start doing pre-recorded reports from across the city. I asked my Madurai Correspondent Sam Daniel to get on a flight and come to Chennai to bolster our coverage.

Sam reached in about 3 hours. We had to wade through knee and neck deep water at several parts of the city. What explained this severe inundation? Widespread encroachments on water bodies was the common refrain of experts. The government was no less culpable. One of my reports was on a government school in Kovilambakkam, built on a lake! Ever year during the monsoon, the playground would be transformed into a huge pool, forcing the poor students to catch fish instead of writing their exams!

The headquarters offered to get me on a helicopter that would cost about a lakh rupees for an hour. But seeing the depth of our coverage, that didn't seem necessary. Sam got on a boat in Pulianthope with dead buffaloes floating around. I managed to get to homes where people were marooned on their terraces; to Corporation relief centres; and to spots where parked vehicles were smashed by fallen trees.

A few months before this, Mumbai had witnessed floods. There was the usual blame game, with celebrities giving quotes on their 'adventures' and newspapers carrying box items on how Amitabh Bachchan was stranded inside his own home and balanced a bottle of coke on his head as he moved from one room to another! The average Mumbaikar vented their spleen at the political top brass for remaining shut inside their cosy official bungalows.

Chennai was quite a contrast. Chief Minister Jayalalithaa was out there, getting her feet wet, inspecting the worst hit areas. Police Commissioner R. Nataraj who was part of the convoy helped me to get access to 'Amma' by pushing me ahead of the surging crowd. Ms. Jayalalithaa noticed me and stopped to answer a few questions.

'Ma'am, is this a failure of our storm water drainage system, year after year?'

'This sort of rainfall is unprecedented. The city's infrastructure is obviously bursting at the seams.'

'Many believe the villain of the piece is encroachment on water bodies.'

'To an extent. We are looking into that aspect and will launch a crackdown soon.'

I called my office to tell them about my proposed story angle – 'A Tale of Two Cities'. News need not always be negative. This was a good example of the official machinery getting its act together, for a change, and of a Chief Minister leading by example.

Sadly, in the months that followed, there was also a tale of two tragedies, with a stampede at relief centres claiming more than 50 lives; a blot on the otherwise good work of the authorities.

The 9 o'clock news had the best bits of our coverage as Sam, the crew and I sat down to have lunch. Yes, lunch at 9 p..! We had our fill of the most meaningful coverage earlier in the day, such that food was the last thing on our minds. By the next day, the NDTV feedback page was flooded with some heart warming comments about our coverage. This more than made up for the paracetamol dose I had missed!

40

WHEN JAYALALITHAA STOPPED HER CONVOY

FEW POLITICAL LEADERS EVOKED as much adulation, fear, awe, and curiosity or stirred up as many controversies as Tamil Nadu's Amma: J. Jayalalithaa. The former film actor turned politician made for great television, given her style of functioning, her political battles and the cases she was mired in. In the late nineties, when I joined NDTV which used to produce the Star News Channel, I had to extensively cover Ms. Jayalalithaa. Although the Bureau Chief Jennifer Arul, who had been her friend for many decades, used to handle the AIADMK beat, and, given my knowledge of spoken Tamil, gained at the Law College, I ended up covering the DMK, there was always news from Amma's camp on Jennifer's off days.

The burning issue was Cauvery. And there was that fragile alliance with the BJP-led National Democratic Alliance, whose boat she ultimately rocked, causing the government to fall. A Jayalalithaa assignment, especially at the AIADMK Party Headquarters, invariably meant jostling with a massive crowd and security personnel who would sometimes fiddle with your rib cage, quite like playing a harp, if they felt you would break the security cordon. On one occasion, I got a taste of this treatment, as I inched forward in a bid to ask Ms. Jayalalithaa a question on the constitution of the Cauvery River Authority. A safari-suit-clad security officer dragged me back by the loop of my belt. Sensing my discomfort, Ms. Jayalalithaa immediately instructed them to allow me to come forward so that I could interact with her without any hassle. 'Are you hurt? Are you OK?' she asked me in a tone that showed genuine concern. It was probably the first time she noticed me, but that was my first impression of her.

True to her convent education, she would always wish you in return, even if it was a crowd and you were not visible. Several times I have witnessed her looking in the direction from where the 'Good Morning Ma'am' emanated and warmly acknowledging it. The same courtesy was evident in the way she handled her correspondence. Almost every letter that I wrote to her elicited a reply. They were not in the round robin cut-copy-paste format but with a personal touch. On one of her birthdays, I sent her a card with a small note inside informing her that I had completed 10 years in NDTV. In 72 hours, I got a reply thanking me for the birthday wishes and adding that it was 'nice to learn that I had, albeit unwittingly, played a role in shaping your career as a TV journalist. My best wishes are with you and your family always.' The warmth in such letters brought out a very different side of a politician who was known to rule with an iron hand.

Elections often afforded the opportunity for closer interaction with political bigwigs. In the run up to the 2011 Assembly Poll, I joined Ms. Jayalalithaa's campaign trail. Emerging from her hotel in Trichy, she acknowledged my request for an interview, routed through my friend Sriram, who was providing her inputs on the electoral scene.

'Got your letter. Thanks,' she told me at the lobby and went on to wave to her party workers. As some of her party colleagues like O. Paneerselvam and Sengottaiyan bowed before her, she got into her campaign van and drove away. I jumped into my car and followed the convoy. An hour later, as I was shooting a Piece to Camera, I was suddenly surrounded by her security officers who shouted in Tamil '*Amma Kupidraanga*' (Amma is calling you); I noticed Ms. Jayalalithaa smiling at me.

'Yes, Sanjay. What are you shooting?'

'Follow the Leader, Ma'am.'

'Sure. You can ask a few questions.'

I managed a quick tête-à-tête on her manifesto and the issues in the election. Soon, the crowd got restive and she had to wrap up the interview.

There were many decisions of hers that we had criticised on the channel: from the dismissal of over a lakh government employees to the slapping of defamation cases against journalists. Although I used to cover her arch rivals – the DMK – extensively, not once did it alter the way she treated me. If I'm not mistaken, I was the first journalist to ask her about her Prime Ministerial ambitions. 'No comments. But thank you for the compliment,' was all that she said with a smile. During an interview in his car, the then Union Minister Dayanidhi Maran brought this up with me. 'Sanjay, I remember you asking her about becoming PM and she seemed to like it. Otherwise, why would she have viewed it as a compliment?' When even single MP parties had managed Ministerial berths at the Centre in the past, a leader of her stature with 37 seats in the Lok Sabha in 2014 could have easily played King Maker or, even become the Queen herself in a coalition government, had the BJP not won a comfortable majority.

A journalist is expected to play an adversarial role. But calling a spade a spade involves also giving credit where it was due, be it the Rainwater Harvesting Scheme, the elimination of the Veerappan menace, the handling of the Tsunami or the Chennai Deluge of 2005, where I witnessed her wading through ankle deep water on an inspection of the city's inundated areas. R. Nataraj, the then Commissioner of Police and now the Mylapore MLA was part of her convoy and had helped me to reach her on one of the stopovers. Which is why I was surprised when she didn't stir out during the Floods in 2015. In hindsight, we know it was her health that prevented her from doing an encore.

After a meeting with BJP partriarch and former Deputy Prime Minister L.K. Advani at the Secretariat in 2012, I was taken aback when Ms. Jayalalithaa called out for me, 'Where's Pinto? Sanjay Pinto.'

It was to thank me for putting out a fair and balanced review of her year in office. That post-press-conference interaction went live. My former NDTV colleague and the then Media Advisor to the Prime Minister Pankaj Pachauri sent me a text message asking why the Chief Minister had asked for me. There were journalist colleagues who began to joke: 'So are you getting a Rajya Sabha ticket?' I did not put that clip out in the public domain at the time. However, after her demise, I posted it on the social media to show the world the humane side of the 'Iron Lady'.

These were not PR stunts to keep journalists in good humour. Well after I left NDTV to plunge into law practice, I was chatting with my friend, the then Additional Commissioner of Police (Chennai South) Rajesh Das near Jayalalithaa's Poes Garden residence. As her convoy drove up to the gate, the top cop had to say a hurried bye and moved forward to salute her. I retreated. On seeing me, Ms. Jayalalithaa stopped her convoy and signalled to me. 'Yes, Sanjay. I don't see you nowadays. How are you? How is your family?' It was then that I informed her that I had quit journalism to become a lawyer. 'Oh lawyer,' she asked as her eyes lit up, having nursed an ambition to become one herself. 'I was not aware. But why?' I then told her how I wanted more time with my family. And to earn more money! She smiled and wished me well. 'We'll meet soon.' I later came to know that she had asked a senior party colleague about my lawyer avatar but I was not sure what she had in mind or what feedback she got. That was the last time I had met her, although I saw her at her swearing-in after a historic consecutive victory in 2016 and the Global Investors Meet, to which her office sent across special invitations. The envelope read: 'Sanjay Pinto, Former NDTV Editor. Now an Advocate.' So it was never the tag; it was the person.

Through her 75-day hospitalisation, I kept praying for her recovery. When she finally passed away, the loss seemed very personal. I was glued to the TV all day, watching the funeral live on Jaya TV. Here was a leader who clearly departed ahead of her time, and before a possible role in national politics.

41

THE GLASS IS CLEANER

'COMMERCIAL PLUG': THE DAY I joined NDTV in February 1998, I was introduced to this term and strictly told to guard against this 'sin' in all forms of reporting and anchoring. An integral part of the organisation's Code of Conduct revolved around the dictum of the Roys that there must be a 'Chinese Wall' between Editorial and Marketing. We in the bureaus took it very seriously. Before every new car launch or business press conference, we were schooled not to accept gifts or favours or junkets of any kind. If companies provided accomodation and travel, NDTV would always turn it down and pay for the crew. (With media houses bleeding today, I'm not sure if this is still the practice; or even feasible.) Even files and pens were left behind, after only pulling out the press release. Soon companies began to feel offended when even diaries and folders were returned. So Jennifer Arul introduced a system of raffling these low value items in the Chennai office. The goal was twofold: to ensure that the Reporters or Camerapersons would not be too keen to collect them at press conferences and also to ensure rotation so that others in the office would also get a chance to 'win' a prize. It was a fair arrangement and worked well.

A school junior of mine and former national rifle shooting champion Girish Ramdas, had come up with a smash proof glass as a security feature for windows and car windscreens. As it was billed as a tool to keep people safe from crime, the launch took place at the Police Commissioner's office. Girish was also the son of veteran IAS officer Mr. C.N. Ramdas. A demonstration was held with the media given hockey sticks and clubs to test the 'unbreakable' glass.

To me, it came across as a nice 'And Finally' story with the scope for an interesting Piece to Camera, that I always loved doing. Facing the camera with a hockey stick in my hand, I turned around and whacked the glass with all my might. One, two, three hard blows; it did not break. I turned back to the camera and said: 'People in glass houses can now start throwing stones at others...'

I filed the story that evening. It was held for the next day's 'Good Morning India' Breakfast Show. The top bosses in Delhi had access to all the scripts mailed. Late that night, I saw an email response from Dr. Prannoy Roy. It read: 'Isn't this a plug for the company?' The mail was marked to a group. Honestly, I was rattled but responded with my explanation pronto.

'Dear Dr. Roy, I beg to differ. I have not mentioned the name of the company anywhere, not in the script, designation of the owner, or even the anchor link. I felt it was a valid story that fitted into 'a changing India' genre we were asked to scout for. And there is an interesting PTC!' I hit the 'Reply All' button. In a few minutes, there were calls from colleagues who wondered if it was right to openly disagree with the Chairman on a group mail. But I was confident with my justification of the story.

By the evening, Amitabh Revi who was the anchor in the studio, called to say that my story was being aired. 'Daddy has replied.' (Prannoy is affectionately called daddy in the office.) This was before the Blackberry era, so as I was not in the office, I could not see the mail.

'What has he replied?' I asked Amitabh.

Dr. Roy's reply was: 'OK, if you're convinced, I am. Full faith.'

I punched my fist up in the air. It was just another reaffirmation of the democracy and freedom employees in NDTV enjoyed, even to the point of openly disagreeing with the founder. The grace with which Dr. Roy responded has made me remember those lines verbatim, even after more than a decade and a half. His faith in his team was unbreakable.

42

GANGSTER'S WIFE

WELL BEFORE HE ELIMINATED the Veerappan menace, top cop K. Vijaykumar was out on a 'Clean Up' mission to rid Chennai of gangs. The city had witnessed a series of 'encounters' in which gangsters fell to police bullets. Although in television journalism, you did not have the luxury of specialising in a beat but had to pretty much cover everything that happened, my childhood fascination for the Indian Police Service (IPS) made me lap up crime reporting. My rapport with the top brass of the police sometimes helped in getting that odd scoop or lead over the others.

This was one pre-dawn encounter that I got wind off quite late. It was in an apartment complex opposite my Alma Mater – Loyola College in Nungambakkam, Chennai. The target was Venkatesan Pannaiyar, who in police files, was a dreaded history-sheeter. The cops claimed that he was wanted in cases of murder, extortion and would often convene kangaroo Courts to settle disputes. Most police encounters trigger doubts over whether it was a kill mission or whether it happened in self defence. Venkatesan's death magnified this suspicion. A few in the media were tipped off soon after the encounter. That I was not one among the breaking news brigade this time around, rankled no end.

At the Police Commissioner's briefing, a press note was circulated. Bare details were given out. The operation was led by S.S. Krishnamoorthy, the then Deputy Commissioner of Police, Central Crime Branch (CCB) which fell under a stylish and suave Joint Commissioner of Police, Central Zone, Mithilesh Kumar Jha ('Montu' in police circles) who had served in the Research Analysis Wing (RAW) on deputation with the Central Government. There were stories about the gangster's meeting at a star hotel pub and how he allegedly displayed a pistol. It just wasn't my day. The Police PRO ran out of press release copies. In sheer frustration, I raised my voice: 'What's happening here?' Unlike many print journalists whose deadline was many hours away, my head office kept calling for live reports. The police chief Vijaykumar, who seemed to like me, heard my argument with the PRO and intervened. 'Sanjay, come over to my office for tea and a chat.'

The prospect of inside information could offset a news break miss. Mr. Vijaykumar described the slain gangster Venkatesan's modus operandi. 'He would appear like a phantom,' I recall him telling me as we sipped piping hot tea. There were a few other details shared and I left a lot less disappointed that morning.

Unlike the other encounters, the police, in this case, had to contend with caste. The dead man belonged to the powerful Nadar community down South. Its leaders were in politics, media, films, and even at high echelons in the administration. So it was not just the human rights activists, and some credible ones at that, who protested, but also the Nadar lobby that raised its voice. A condolence meeting was held at Kamaraj Hall, which drew a crowd of a few thousand people. Notable among the audience was a retired Director General of Police who hailed from the same community. Speaker after speaker denounced the police action, vowed to fight it legally and dwelled on Venkatesan's good deeds in his hometown in Southern Tamil Nadu.

The media focus on what the family and supporters of the deceased termed a 'fake encounter', with doubts as to whether he had actually opened fire on the police party or not, what with a report that a revolver seized from the scene of crime, not in a working condition, forced the Tamil Nadu Government under Ms. Jayalalithaa to appoint a Commission of Enquiry under Retired Justice Raman. A petition was filed in the Madras High Court calling for a CBI probe.

Post the encounter, in a dramatic twist of fate, the slain gangster's wife Radhika Selvi was given a ticket by the DMK to contest the Lok Sabha election from the Thiruchendur constituency, a Nadar stronghold. Images of the young widow campaigning with her child in her arms created a wave of sympathy and she won with a comfortable margin. The twist of fate was followed by a masterstroke by party chief

M. Karunanidhi, who sent her name to the UPA alliance for her induction as a Minister of State at the Centre. The portfolio allotted came as a big surprise. Radhika Selvi was made the Minister of State for Home! Although a junior minister, under the seasoned Shivraj Patil, the fact that the police came under her, was like life coming full circle.

Not every minister is interview material. But given these circumstances, my head office jumped at my story idea and even asked me to try to do the interview live. When I met Radhika Selvi, I was quite impressed by her polite and courteous demeanour. After the usual pleasantries and briefing, I looked into the camera and started my introduction. 'Joining me is a gangster's wife, now a Minister who technically controls the police who killed her husband in an encounter...' At this point, she stopped me and said: 'Why do you refer to me as a gangster's wife? I'm a Minister now. My husband's past is debatable. What has been proved against him? The encounter was staged.' There was no anger in her voice but I realised I had touched a raw nerve. The camera rolled afresh. I did not steer clear of the connection but merely resisted the temptation of using the term 'gangster's wife'. Despite being a political novice, the lady came across as quite intelligent and clued in.

On my way back to the bureau, I couldn't help thinking about what she said. Did I sacrifice sensitivity for a juicy introduction? Why should a spouse, that too a woman, in this era of gender bias and stereotypes, be tied down to her husband's chequered past? Even if facts are unpalatable, should a journalist alter an expression on an interviewee's request?

Truth be told, had I not made that change, I would not have got that interview. Would sticking to that 'banned' expression have really mattered to the viewers? Or would they have been content with a glimpse into the mind of a young minister with an uncommon background? These are questions that deserve far deeper introspection. For me, the uplink and the next day's plan beckoned.

43

STICKY WICKET

WHENEVER A VISITING CRICKET team is in an Indian city, the role of the Correspondent in the Bureau is not limited to covering their arrival or net practice and the daily official media briefing. Every channel would try to outshine the other with a surprise exclusive interview with a star player. With a Sports Editor like Gulu Ezekiel, the bar would always be raised higher.

The Pakistan team was in Chennai. Gulu encouraged me to give Wasim Akram a shot. I tried without 'influence' but an interview seemed remote. Gulu worked the phones and put in a word to the Pakistan team physiotherapist Dan Kiesel. Akram was in the middle of an intense stretching session. I waited for him to finish and as he was wrapping up, I reminded Dan about the request.

'Come along. I'll ask Wasim.'

Turning to his frontline bowler, Dan introduced me.

'This is Sanjay Pinto from Star News. He wants to do an interview with you.'

With a straight face, Akram shot back: 'Ask Sanjay Pinto and Star News to go to hell.'

I was taken aback by the needless rudeness. You can decline a request politely. And it was not as if I had disturbed him, as a result of which, he had strained a muscle!

The college debater in me surfaced. 'Sure, Mr. Akram. With you forming a happy trio.' Akram had a smirk. I walked away.

I had thought the interview was a foregone conclusion. But as they say in cricket, nothing is certain till the last delivery. And to me it seemed that when the bowler is Wasim Akram, you may need to be prepared for a swinging yorker or a bouncer. In hindsight, everyone is entitled to a bad day!

As I look back, I realise that while I had interviewed almost all the cricketers from all the countries at some point or the other, I never really enjoyed a good rapport with players from the Pakistan squad. That includes one of their Coaches.

It was the Asia Cup hosted in Sri Lanka in 2004. NDTV had a sponsored interview with a few big names. Bob Woolmer was one of them. The then coach of the Pakistan side was known to speak his mind on the game, no holds barred.

While the teams were staying at the Taj Samudra, I was booked into Trans Asia Hotel, about 5 kilometres away. There were slots fixed in advance for all the interviews. Slots are not always written in stone and a change here or there was absolutely fine.

I had just crashed for the night. It was about 11 p.m. when my mobile phone rang. It was Bob Woolmer on the line.

'Hello. Sanjay, let's finish tomorrow's interview.'

'When, Bob?'

'Right now.'

I didn't like the tone. To wake up someone at that hour without even an apology was bad enough. To summon me with no notice seemed unacceptable. Had I been staying at the same hotel, I could have woken up the cameraperson and gone over to his room. But I was a few kilometres away. A car had to be organised.

'I'm not an ambulance, Bob.' There was silence at the other end.

On second thoughts, I took a deep breath. 'All right; it will take me at least twenty minutes to get there.'

I reached Woolmer's room in about 15 minutes. He was in the middle of his dinner or post-dinner snack. I could see french fries and juice.

We finished the interview. As we were packing up to leave, Woolmer remarked: 'Sorry to have pulled you out of bed, mate. I have to meet someone tomorrow.'

On my way out, I thought to myself. How different is the job of a 24x7 TV journalist from ambulance staff?

44

COLLEAGUE IN CUSTODY

LIKE A FEW PROFESSIONS, journalism can make you rub folks the wrong side by just doing your job. Transport Unions had called for a strike in Chennai. Monitoring the extent to which essential services like hospitals would be hit was an obvious story for a newspaper or television news channel. I had assigned the task to my colleague Sam Daniel with a clear brief to do a reality check at government hospitals. Sam's first stop was the Rajiv Gandhi Government General Hospital diagonally opposite the Chennai Central Railway Station. It was possible to feel the pulse of the public as it were, through a few interviews of patients coming in. Sam was doing just that.

For some inexplicable reason, an Assistant Resident Medical Officer (ARMO) got hot under the collar on spotting a television crew on the campus and decided to ask them to leave. Sam stood his ground, and rightly so. An argument ensued. The government doctor complained about NDTV's presence to the GH Police Outpost. The officials there seemed clueless about the right of the media to enter government buildings and report and in a bizarre move, took Sam and the cameraperson Devaraj to the outpost.

The drill in NDTV was to mention the Expected Time of Arrival (ETA) of edited stories. Well past the story ETA, there was no sign of Sam. His mobile phone was not reachable. For a Correspondent who was always known to meet deadlines, being incommunicado for a few hours made my TV-reporter antennae tingle. All our NDTV cars, hired from Bala Tourist Service, were fitted with walkie talkies. It took a while to reach our driver Mahendran on the wireless. Mahendran too was waiting for the crew to return to have lunch. I requested him to search for Sam. In about half an hour, Mahendran called back to explain what had transpired.

'Sir, the police has detained Sam and Devaraj at the outpost. Some doctor had objected to their shooting interviews.'

This was wrongful confinement and downright illegal, I told myself and made a dash to the GH outpost. I was shocked to find Sam and Devaraj sitting inside on a bench, relieved to see me. They were ordered to switch off their phones and wait for the arrival of the Inspector.

I called Mrs. Letika Saran, the Commissioner of Police. There was no response on her mobile. I left a message with her Camp Clerk. In 2 minutes, the Commissioner rang back.

'Sanjay, what has happened? They have detained your team, is it?'

'Yes, Ma'am. This is unacceptable,' I answered.

'They can leave right away. Let me find out why they did this.'

I thanked her and told the Sub Inspector there that I had spoken to the Commissioner and she had authorised me to take my colleagues out.

Sam almost broke down, deeply hurt by the overreaction of that doctor and the local cops to his legitimate work.

We decided to file a complaint against the doctor. I later heard that he had filed a counter complaint against Sam and had threatened to tear his own shirt to press trumped up charges of assault against my colleagues!

Sam's father was keen on filing an anticipatory bail plea in the Madras High Court. I felt it was not required at all. Senior Journalist R. Bhagwan Singh called to reassure us and express solidarity.

'Sanjay, if Sam is arrested, we will come to the road.'

Bhagwan Singh has always been a champion of media freedom. His support was not surprising and meant a lot to us.

I took Sam along to meet the Joint Commissioner of Police – Mr. Sylendra Babu – the next day. Mr. Babu was a friend of the media and a no-nonsense officer. I also gathered that the Intelligence Section (IS) had filed a speculative report that both sides – the media and government doctors – were planning demonstrations in the city! And all along I thought speculation was the monopoly of the media!

No agitations were conducted. There was no need to, as both sides buried the hatchet. This day in the life of a journalist was not quite what the doctor ordered. Or maybe it was!

45

GOVERNOR PLAYS GUIDE

'MU KARUNANIDHI ENUM NAAN....' (I, M. Karunanidhi...) Tamil Nadu Governor Surjit Singh Barnala had memorised the opening line of the oath that he administered to M. Karunanidhi as he swore him in as Chief Minister in 2006. To those familiar with Tamil Nadu politics, this was more than a Kodak moment. It was a reflection of the affection and respect Barnala had for Karunanidhi, whose DMK government he refused to dismiss under Article 356 of the Constitution in 1991, and chose to put in his papers instead. Life came full circle when the veteran Shiromani Akali Dal leader got a chance to see his friend in office again in 2006. Which is why the smattering of Tamil that he had picked up and expressed at the swearing-in ceremony drew applause. Newspapers carried box items the next day. But no one had got a response from the Governor on his equation with the DMK patriarch. It was not of great political significance but certainly a matter of interest.

Hearing about the rapport between the two leaders from the horse's mouth was always on my mind. In May, 2006, NDTV had an opt-out experiment with 'Southern Edition', a news bulletin exclusively on South India, anchored by some of us in Chennai, Hyderabad, Bengaluru and Thiruvananthapuram. as well as a weekly half-hour chat show from these regions, 'Chennai Talkies', was meant for interviews with film stars. I made an exception for Governor Barnala. My request for a 'walk the talk' found prompt acceptance, although the octogenarian could not be expected to walk for too long. I began with the 'Mu Karunanidhi Enum Naan' line. Barnala smiled and took the cue.

'We are almost the same age. Karunanidhi is a year older. He is my good friend and although we may have certain ideological differences, our bonding is quite strong. I enjoy his political satire and wit.' I noticed how Barnala was able to pronounce the title '*Kalaignar*' used to address Karunanidhi, like a true blue Tamilian.

'By differences, you mean the DMK's demand to scrap the post of Governor?' I couldn't resist that question.

'That and other issues. You see, I am in public life but out of active politics.'

I prodded him on the Tamil oath of office.

'Usually people from outside the State learn to say *Vanakkam*. I just went a step ahead! To identify with the people of the State was the idea. That it was for a long standing friend was coincidental.'

As I was shooting the interview, I got a routine call from my Delhi office to ask about the story for the day. I informed the Input Desk that I was doing Chennai Talkies with Barnala. The idea didn't pass muster with my headquarters as the bosses felt a chat with an 80-year-old constitutional figurehead would dilute the 'glamour quotient' of the programme aimed at TRPs. The editorial reservations surfaced in an email just while I was wrapping up the interview! I had to ignore the objection.

Barnala opened up and gave me a guided tour of the Raj Bhavan himself. This included a trip to his art gallery as his grandson Ajeshwar joined in.

'Today, I can hardly walk. But I was up to quite a bit in my younger days! There were at least three attempts on my life by Pakistan-trained terrorists. Do you know how I once escaped from my home in Chandigarh? By disguising my appearance. I managed to give militants who were looking for me, the slip. A Sikh can easily change his appearance by dyeing his beard and changing the way his turban is tied!'

Some of the stories he shared, particularly the ones off-camera were rivetting. The session ended in tea and cookies. I waited for Barnala to take the first sip but ended up with a singed lip as it was piping hot. Evidently, my host was so accustomed to drinking really hot beverages that I could have nicknamed him 'Burnol-a'!

The bigger challenge was to get the bosses for whom this interview was not their cup of tea, to change their mind. My trump card, as it were, was Sreenivasan Jain, to whom I confided and he interceded for me. By that evening, the green signal came through, with a strict instruction to stick only to movie stars for Chennai Talkies. I agreed. But couldn't help thinking about a biopic on veteran leaders, both alive and deceased, for a special programme someday.

46

SOUND OF SILENCE

WHAT THEY PROBABLY DON'T teach you at Journalism School is the art of entering a jam-packed room for an interview or press conference. But if you've been baptised in the sweat of Dravidian land, it gets competitive.

A.R. Rahman was on a roll. After the Golden Globes and BAFTA, he scored a hat-trick with two Oscar Awards. The Mozart of Chennai always returned to a rousing welcome at the Chennai Airport and his home. Capturing the celebration – the frenzied fans, the beating of drums, folk artistes, garlands and music – of course, made for great television. Never mind the midnight arrival; never mind the fact that television journalists had already worked the whole day and the clock was reset again after a hurried dinner. The anticipation also had to be covered live. Such was the saturation coverage planned for the return of India's pride in music.

I had covered the previous two arrivals. But this was the Oscars; it justifiably doesn't get bigger. The scene at the Chennai Airport was predictable. Fans, curious passengers, onlookers and journalists, all jostling for not just space but a vantage point to stick a mike out, click pictures, or shoot video footage of the hero's welcome.

Murphy's Law invariably takes over and delays the arrival of flights. This night was no exception.

Rahman has always been a simple and down to earth soul, whose humility seemed to go up with every new feat. After obliging the photographers and the sound bite collectors right outside the arrival point, he was bundled into his car. A battery of students, troupe members, fans and media persons formed an impromptu convoy from the airport to Rahman's Kodambakkam home in Chennai.

It's not easy being a celebrity newsmaker. An Oscar award winner just back home, after already having spoken to the media at the Airport could have jolly well excused himself and spent time with his family or just crashed. But that's not how A.R. Rahman is made.

There was a near-stampede at his home. I thought the glass door would be shattered. In such situations, the first crew in usually gets the first shot at an exclusive interview, not necessarily a sit-down tête-à-tête but what in television parlance is called a 'tic-tac' with the subject standing. Each TV channel gets about three to five minutes of what is later hyped as an 'exclusive' interview. National TV channels are often the first in the pecking order, unless local considerations catapult favourite regional players ahead.

I was among the first to get a chance. Just as I shook hands with Rahman and got his nod for the interview, I discovered, to my chagrin, that my NDTV 24x7 cameraperson Sagayaraj was not inside the room. A newcomer from our fledgling sister channel NDTV Hindu, which was then in the process of doing trial runs, had managed to get in instead. As there was no time to search for Sagayaraj, I just went ahead and shot the interview with the junior cameraman. It was a nice chat with Rahman even holding up the two Oscars and proclaiming: 'I dedicate this to the youth of India.' I knew this would be that classic headline shot with a breathe of those words.

Getting out of the venue that was bursting at the seams was as challenging as getting in. Emerging finally from that room at that hour, I must have been quite a sight. I bumped into singer Chinmayi, who had also come to congratulate Rahman. We chatted a bit while looking for our drivers.

It was about 3 a.m. when I reached the Chennai Bureau. The interview had to be uplinked to Delhi so that it could run in the first bulletin of the morning at six. Imagine my horror when it became evident that there was no audio in the main channel. The junior cameraperson, in that melee, had recorded the interview with the camera mike and not the gun mike as he was supposed to. The camera mike is meant only to record what we call 'nat sounds' and not the main interview. The uplinked version therefore had muffled audio throughout. Working through the night just for this sound of silence? 'Tomorrow is another day' is easier said than done, especially when it happens to someone else.

The Video Editors in Delhi did their best to correct the audio by boosting it but it was still not normal. The importance of the interview lay not just in the news value but also the fact that all the other channels too had it. As they were all 'exclusive interviews', it could not be borrowed as, say, general sound bites or press conferences.

I shot off a mail to the Editors in Delhi about what had transpired. In what was a consolation, the interview was aired as a headline. But as I have always believed, if it does not run on prime time, you've not quite made it. The bad audio was a perfect reason to redo it! Even without such production glitches, there is this practice called the 'mock live' or 'Sim Sat' (simulated satellite), that I have found unethical and unfair. Essentially, the interviewee is asked a set of questions by the correspondent and instead of looking at the interviewer on the spot, he looks straight into the camera. The questions are then emailed to the prime time anchor, fed into the tele-prompter and made to appear that they were asking Rahman those questions live!

On many occasions, if you happen to watch prime time news in a TV showroom or airport with multiple screens, you will end up seeing the same person on different channels live at the same time! Who says newsmakers can't be omnipresent!

Life has a way of rubbing disappointments in.

A few friends who had watched the 'live' interview had a legitimate question. 'Sanjay, you didn't do that big interview with Rahman?'

My answer just had to be: 'Yes. And No.'

Or I should have, a la Simon and Garfunkel, broken into song:

'People talking without watching...

People rolling without recording...

People nodding without interviewing....

People conducting interviews that channels never share...

On Prime Time.

No one dared to question the Sound of Silence.'

47

A FIAT AND AN AMBASSADOR

FIRING THE FIRST SALVO at press conferences was a habit I had cultivated over the years. Honestly, it made my job easier because I would know exactly where my answer was on the tape obviating the need to sift through an hour's footage to cue to what I wanted. Sometimes it also unwittingly created an 'impression'! Little did I realise that asking former American President and the then UN Envoy Bill Clinton the first question during his interaction with the media at the Chennai Airport, as part of a tsunami reconstruction initiative, would send the right signals!

'Mr. Clinton, the Prime Minister of India says we should work towards converting disaster into opportunity. How do you see that happening?'

Dressed in a casual T-shirt and cotton trousers Clinton smiled and went on to answer that elaborately for almost

5 minutes! After the press conference, a US Consulate official walked up to me and asked for my visiting card. I handed it over and forgot about what was, at one level, just another media briefing. A couple of days later, a contact in the Consulate told me that my style – of putting my hand up and shooting the first poser that was brief and pointed – went down well with the bosses! Brownie points, eh?! But I wasn't looking for a US Visa or a junket and in fact had politely declined two consecutive offers of an all-expenses paid trip for a Young Leaders Fellowship in the United States.

Long after I moved on a sort of deputation from the mother channel to editorially head NDTV Hindu, there was a call from the US Consulate.

Indian-born American officer Anand Krishna was on the line, 'Hi Sanjay. How are you doing? Just calling to offer you an exclusive interview with Ambassador Timothy Roemer who is coming down to Chennai the day after tomorrow.'

'Thank you, Anand. But you are aware that I'm not with NDTV 24x7 now. I'm with NDTV Hindu. We are a Chennai-centric channel! Would it make sense for you?'

'Absolutely, it would. A lot of expats are regular viewers of your channel. And the Consulate has picked you for the interview!'

'Oh that's great. Happy to do this, Anand! Where? At what time?'

'Ambassador Roemer will have an informal chat with a select group of journalists at the American International School, that's pretty close to your office in Perungudi (I hope I got that right!) If you can please come there at 10 o'clock, we will fix a 5-to-10-minute exclusive sit-down with you.'

'Yes, Anand. I'll be there.'

There were just a handful of journalists; about eight or ten. The North East monsoon had set in and I wondered what Mr. Roemer would have thought about the road leading to the American School, that resembled a war zone with not just potholes but craters.

The top diplomat arrived well on time and, after being introduced to the gathering effortlessly began chatting with everyone almost as if he was catching up with old friends. The man is an extrovert, I thought to myself. As I was introduced, he started singing hosannas about NDTV's 'Save the Tiger' campaign.

The timing of this interaction was significant. It was just after President Obama's visit to India, the day after the Wikileaks cables on India were leaked and on the anniversary of the Bhopal Gas Tragedy and the ongoing furore over the inability to extradite Union Carbide head honcho Warren Anderson.

I had taken cameramen Sagayaraj and Madhan along. Even before our slot, the duo had zeroed in on a suitable background for the interview.

The general briefing done, Anand came up to me. 'Sanjay, five to ten minutes ok? We start in two minutes.'

I had made mental notes of all the main issues that would make news, coming from the US Ambassador.

'Yes, Sanjay. Are we ready to go? Check one, two, three...'

That was Mr. Roemer as soon as he sat down and adjusted his tie.

My opening reference made him smile like a child!

'My interviewee was first person President Obama hugged on landing on Indian soil.'

That could have sounded like a bait, because I soon subjected him to a barrage of the most difficult questions and was mentally prepared for him to even walk out of the interview at some point.

'Are you embarrassed by the WikiLeaks trove of US diplomatic correspondence. How damaging is it?'

Having served as a Congressman on the House Intelligence Committee and a member of the 9/11 Commission, Mr. Roemer was presented with a generous dose of posers on Pakistan. The questions ranged from India's legitimate demand to bring the perpetrators of 26/11 to justice, to the Cold Start Doctrine; from the US interest in India's military strategy, to whether America is batting for Pakistan; and even on Anne Patterson's communication in 2009 on the US need to reassess military sales to India as it may feed Pakistan's paranoia and push them closer to both Afghan and Kashmir-focussed terror groups.

The Ambassador was unruffled and didn't sound diplomatic in his replies! My 'five-to-ten' minutes were up a while back but as he showed no sign of wanting to leave, so I persisted with more queries: on the US take on the war crimes against Tamils in Sri Lanka; on America losing the FIFA bid to Qatar that's as small as the population of San Francisco; on whether not visiting the Taj Mahal, unlike French President Sarkozy, was President Obama's loss; and on when his leader would come back to India. Mr. Roemer seemed so relaxed and comfortable that on more than a couple of occasions, he referred to Obama as 'my friend'. By the time I finished, it was almost half-an-hour!

'Thank you for your time, for the extra time Mr. Roemer! You are an interviewer's delight!' I genuinely meant it.

'You're most welcome, Sanjay. You asked all the right questions. I didn't expect some of them! I had also come to your city to watch my son face some beamers at a baseball match. I got a few too! Good job. Pleasure.'

As he got ready to leave, I mentioned that an uncle of mine – Kenneth Shivers – was a diplomat and had worked as a Vice Consul in Chennai when I was a little boy.

'Oh, so you have some American blood in you!'

'Not really. But even without that, I would love to shake hands with your 'friend' some day!'

'Well, all things are possible! See you. Take care.'

I aired the whole interview on my show 'Corridors of Power'. But as it centred around international relations with three or four hard news pegs, I sent the entire transcript to NDTV 24x7. Senior Managing Editor Sonia Singh, who was on leave but was still checking mails wrote back saying, 'great to get him.'

I'm not sure how much of that interview was used on the national channel. Now, how did I forget that I was from the Republic of South India?!

48

THE LIGHTHOUSE SHOOK

AFTER A SABBATICAL, THE scheduled commencement of my third innings at NDTV – as the Resident Editor – at the start of the new financial year in 2012, was advanced by a day, due to a big political development that erupted in Tamil Nadu. The political temperature gradually died down. However, there was no let up in nature's eruptions and faultlines. It was 11 April. I had just picked up my wife from IIT Madras and was on the way home for lunch when I started getting text messages from viewers about tremors felt in parts of Chennai. Soon my mobile phone rang. A voice from the Delhi Input Desk shrieked: 'Sanjay, tsunami warning! We need you live right now!' There was a massive earthquake in Northern Sumatra measuring more than 8 on the Richter scale, triggering a tsunami warning to 28 countries. India was somewhere at the top of the list. It revived memories of the killer waves that had ravaged coastal Tamil Nadu in 2004, claiming more than 7000 lives. Obviously, this was a potentially huge story especially for television channels, what with the earlier lessons learnt.

I instructed the Live OB Van Crew stationed at the NDTV Bureau in C.I.T. Colony to rush to Marina Beach. My mobile phone kept ringing, beeping with message notifications as I honked my way to the office, parked my car. and jumped into an autorickshaw. The OB Van was positioned near the Lighthouse, one of the city's best known landmarks, and the signal was just up when I reached the spot a little past 2:45 p.m. The initial eyewitness accounts of panic were reflected in my first couple of live reports. I then asked our OB Engineer Suresh if the van cable would reach the top of the Lighthouse. 'Yes,' he said with an air of excitement. The herd mentality is not alien to media operations. So as a few of us hit upon the idea of attempting a nice aerial view from the Lighthouse, almost 75 other reporters and camerapersons and photographers followed suit. Due to the tremors, power was switched off, so we had to clamber up nine floors lugging heavy equipment. The rather small balcony atop the ninth floor was suddenly bursting at the railings. What was designed for probably ten people to stand was filled with about 50 of us. The thought of the balcony crashing down had to be quickly banished from our mind if we had to concentrate on the coverage. It was a vantage point to capture the killer waves. We waited with bated breath, still recovering from the exhaustion of climbing up and awaiting nature's fury.

All of a sudden, we looked at each other.

'Did you feel that?' I asked cameraperson Edwin.

'*Macha*, run *da*, run...'

There were quake aftershocks and we felt as if the Lighthouse was swaying! I ripped off the live ear piece connected to the audio cable and, as I scampered down for dear life, I pressed the Input Desk number on my speed dial.

'After shocks; the Lighthouse was swaying...' I mumbled, still trying to catch my breath. The voice at the other end seemed unruffled.

'Can you quickly uplink visuals of the Lighthouse swaying?'

Now, these are occasions when the disconnect between the desk (not everyone but a few, at least) and reality hits home even harder.

Just in case the cameraperson had kept rolling as he rushed down, I checked with him before responding to the desk.

'We don't have those pictures.'

It elicited a stern. 'Why, that would have been dramatic footage *yaar*!'

'Because our lives were a little more important than your dramatic footage, *yaar*,' I shot back.

Back on terra firma, shaken but not stirred by that strange request, I decided to focus on the impending disaster tourism angle. Although there were deaths of beach go-ers in 2004 when the tsunami struck, it didn't deter folks from displaying misplaced bravado by venturing out towards the water. The local police started making announcements asking the public to keep away from the shores but, quite like the waves, they just kept coming back! I shot a pre-recorded chat with a few of those 'bravehearts'.

'Aren't you scared? Why are you standing here? Isn't your life at stake?'

'In 2004, I just missed it, Sir. That's why I have come back today.'

'Just missed what? Death?'

'Photo, Sir! I also have a new mobile phone.'

'You mean you're not scared of the tsunami but you just want that photo? You should join NDTV!'

A smart alec came up with a repartee. 'Mr. Pinto, why are you standing here with your camera?'

'That's my job. To keep viewers informed. And hopefully, youngsters like you away from danger.'

As the police finally managed to shoo away all the curious onlookers, I had only a few fishermen for company.

'There is a warning of another tsunami...' Even before I could complete my sentence, an elderly fisherman cut me short.

'*Saar*, tsunami *varum*, *aannaal varaadhu*,' (The tsunami will come but it won't!)

The gut feel of these folks who worship the sea, is arguably more accurate than the forecasts of scientists and meteorologists. Almost on cue, the tsunami warning was lifted. Throughout this period, my wife Vidya kept texting updates on the power coming back, my reports being aired and that she and our twin babies were safe at home. I must admit that these updates helped me keep my composure and concentration intact.

NDTV was the only TV channel remaining on the Marina Beach. All the others had packed up and left. The prime time bulletins had obviously slotted the tsunami scare as top story.

Normalcy had returned. As TV is all about pictures, just before the 8 p.m. news, I spotted a small boy with a choco-bar ice-cream on the beach. I invited him with his family to join the show as guests. That visual of the boy licking his ice cream would tell the story of normalcy better than any lofty peroration from yours truly. I would have bought one for myself and had it on air but for a vow that I had made to give up chocolate for life when my kids were born. But there was a better treat for me in store at the end of an eventful day. An email from the Editorial Director Sonia Singh: 'Just great to have you back, Sanjay.'

But she did not say, for how long; that would have been prophetic.

49

WARDROBE BLUES

MARK TWAIN'S GEM 'I never let my schooling interfere with my education' rings true for the top notch actor, Kamal Haasan, more than anyone else. A class Eight school dropout, is quite an intellectual giant. An interview with him would be quite a lesson in itself. Candid and articulate, I have always been in awe of his repartee. There was another trait that came to the fore in another interview.

In what turned out to be my last interview with him for NDTV, I had approached '*Ullaganayagan*' or 'Global Star' as he is called by his fans, in 2010, for an exclusive sit down days ahead of his movie *Manmadhan Ambu* ('Cupid's Arrow') opposite the vivacious Trisha. This romantic comedy did reasonably well at the box office. Kamal's office in Alwarpet is a landmark in Chennai and is equipped with a preview theatre and several backdrops ideal for shooting. There was a montage of hundreds of his film roles right from his introduction into the industry as a child artiste.

My cameraperson sized up the locations and decided to steer clear of the usual settings in certain rooms and instead zeroed in on a location near the renovated dining area on the first floor. The interiors were bright and looked like it had been recently done up. A little birdie revealed that it had actor Gautami's personal touch.

For a seasoned star, Kamal Haasan could have jolly well shot down the interview frame and insisted on his chosen spots. It is in these little matters that a person's real stature becomes evident. Although he looked a tad surprised on seeing the set up, he did not question the cameraperson's decision or suggest an alternative. But that was not all.

Clad in a pale blue shirt, he sat in front of the camera and put on his lapel microphone. I sensed that my cameraperson was uneasy and constantly doing a 'white balance' with the thermocol that the crew carries on shoots, to get the colour right. Kamal was ready and we began chatting off the record. I asked him if he had ever used botox, if he indulged in biriyani from Samco Hotel next door.

'Botox would give you a slightly masked appearance. So, that's a 'No' for me. Biriyani, yes, once in a way.'

The cameraperson slowly whispered into my ears.

'Sanjay, his shirt is not good. It's too light. Can we ask him to change it?'

'Eh, he was surprised about your location choice. Now to change his shirt? Hmmm. Ok.'

'Mr. Haasan, your shirt seems to be burning on camera. Is it possible to change it?'

Without batting an eyelid, he got up, left the set and was back in 2 minutes in a different shirt. But this was light pink! If you are thinking what I was thinking, we were both right! The cameraperson found this shade worse than the earlier colour.

'You're going to hate me for this. But do you have a solid, dark colour shirt?'

'Sure. Give me a minute. I've done this in films before. First time for a TV interview.' he chuckled and was back in a jiffy sporting a black shirt. I was never so relieved to see a person in a black shirt before!

The interview lasted longer than what I had asked for, with no celebrity tantrums. Despite the provocation, Kamal Haasan did not lose his shirt over the need to change the colours, recognising the fact that the man behind the lens is the boss.

This wasn't a one-off indication of his down-to-earth demeanour. In August 2009, my wife Vidya who is an ardent fan of the actor, had sent him a long review of his hit film *Hey Ram*. It was an academically researched piece and not like run-of-the-mill fan mail. In a couple of days, Kamal responded with a two-page letter. 'Some of the symbols you have understood precisely as intendedwarm my heart (sic). I must confess some gain greater value than I had intended with your textual explanations.' Vidya has preserved that letter along with her degrees and marksheets, a reflection of the value and impact of that communication. Talk of being a school dropout, eh!

50

CONTENT SUCCESSFUL, CHANNEL DEAD

IN MOST PROFESSIONS, JOB descriptions change with job titles. A senior doctor does not do what he started off with as a house surgeon: administering injections, preparing discharge summary notes or working in shifts in the ICU. A senior advocate does not get adjournments or appear in trial courts for routine, non-effective hearings, and for that matter, does not sign *vakalat*s. A senior cricketer does not carry drinks to the field; a Police Commissioner does not draw up First Information Reports or flag down motorists who jump signals. But in television journalism, if you are in a Bureau, away from the Headquarters, you will continue to perform tasks a Cub Reporter would do: getting vox pops as inputs for a country wide story such as responses from citizens at petrol pumps on price hikes; live reports on a heat wave; get frenzied fans on camera during a live telecast of a cricket match; or worse, stand at New Year Party bashes and wax eloquent on how folks are celebrating. It falls under 'Team Work'. I am not referring to a big news story like a terror strike or a rail accident or death of a big leader, where the top editors would obviously be on the field. My point is restricted to the daily grind.

Stagnation is an occupational hazard of a journalist in the bureaus. The first time I was allowed near the anchor's chair was when 'Southern Edition' – NDTV's new Opt Out experiment – was launched. At 7:30 p.m., a special half-hour show exclusively on South India, with local anchor-driven discussions and live reports, would be beamed only in the four Southern State Capitals – Chennai, Bengaluru, Hyderabad and Thiruvananthapuram – while the rest of the country would watch the regular 'national' programming. Like all good things, this show did not last too long. And the transition from a reporter to a news anchor continued to be inexplicably out of bounds for the bureaus. When I once raised this with Dr. Prannoy Roy, he flashed that charming smile and retorted: 'Sanjay, I too have been doing the same thing for decades!" Dr. Roy was both right and wrong: right because he is still doing what he started off with, which was anchoring flagship shows; wrong because in my case, a natural progression from reporting was anchoring. And that proved to be quite elusive.

Unlike certain channels, NDTV never had the concept of 'newsreaders', who had to merely parrot what was on the teleprompter. A seasoned Reporter graduated to an anchor with an understanding of how news unfolded and a capacity to handle back-to-back bulletins with breaking news, even without a teleprompter. So it was never an issue of powdering your nose and showing your face on TV. Anchoring was a sign of having arrived. And it did not signal the end of field reporting, which continued to be a part of your job description on days you were not rostered for the studio.

Sometime in 2008, I had got wind of NDTV's soon-to-be-launched Chennai-centric news and features channel, as a joint venture with *The Hindu* newspaper. It was to be christened NDTV Hindu. I had put up my hand for a senior editorial role here but the bosses shot down the idea of a shift from the national channel to a local one, terming it a 'demotion'. I gave up the idea and, in a few months, bitten by the entrepreneurial bug, I had reworked my working relationship with NDTV, ceased to be an employee, and became a Consultant. This gave me the freedom to write a column for *The Hindu* and host a debate show on the city's only English Radio Station, Chennai Live 104.8 FM, owned by the Muthoot Group.

Towards the end of 2009, destiny took over and the editorial mantle of NDTV Hindu was offered to me. Having moved on, I was initially reluctant to get back to the news grind. After a great deal of thought, I accepted the offer to be its Executive Editor but only as a Consultant and not an employee. Barring the hosting of the flagship weekly debate show 'Chennai Speaks Out', the CEO Rajiv Lulla wanted me to focus on building the news bulletins, rather than getting 'sidetracked with anchoring commitments.' This meant writing questions for cub reporters who were asked to anchor discussions. On one occasion, Paul

Kannagaraj, the President of the Madras High Court Advocates Association, who was a panellist, asked the young anchor a counter question and she was stumped! I used that incident to gently illustrate to the young team the need to do research themselves, and to hone skills like ad-libbing and coming up with their own repartees.

The 'behind the scenes' work description did not last beyond a few months and I was soon at liberty to do as much anchoring as I wanted. It was like being placed in a chocolate factory with the freedom to eat as much as you want. Chances are that you would end up nibbling rather than hogging. And so it was with anchoring on NDTV Hindu. I chose to anchor prime time bulletins on big news nights or during the day for breaking news and encouraged the youngsters in the team to occupy the anchor chair with regular practice with the autocue machine. For the first time in the country, even interns were given a chance to anchor a few non-primetime live bulletins. What I did not get in my formative years, I was determined to give others. In a sense, the thirst for the anchor chair was satiated with the biblical logic: 'He who exalts himself shall be humbled. And he who humbles himself shall be exalted!'

My two-year stint with NDTV Hindu gave me the sort of exposure I had always wanted and thought I deserved. The editorial independence the channel enjoyed was too good to be true. Despite the joint venture with the *Hindu*, Mr. N. Ram the Editor-in-Chief of the newspaper and a close friend of Dr. Roy, did not interfere with a single story or bulletin. Not one call or message to ask us to cover or drop a story. The only time he communicated was when I would text him the weekly TRP ratings for the channel. On good weeks, Mr. Ram would be quick to congratulate the team through an SMS. My respect for this doyen of journalism shot up during this period. In 2010, I met the then Managing Director of the paper Mr. K. Balaji to seek his support for publicity for the channel. The response was tremendous and a quarter page colour advertisement was sanctioned for NDTV Hindu every Sunday on Page 2!

Despite the goodwill from some quarters, the odds were against NDTV Hindu in many ways. Frankly, there was no other channel that could be pitted against it to compare ratings. It was then the only Chennai-centric English news channel. The other regional 'competitors' were Tamil channels. So it got bracketed with the national channels with much greater distribution and marketing muscle, and TRPs were viewed along with them. The channel was not available on DTH platforms like Tata Sky. Viewers had to switch on NDTV 24x7 and then press a Red Button on the screen to watch NDTV Hindu as a Picture in Picture. While the target audience was the upwardly mobile, young viewer, who would watch TV on DTH platforms, we were not available there. This was a killer. Poor distribution meant skimpy marketing. The average television viewer in Chennai seemed to prefer national content. For local stuff, there were newspapers and vernacular TV channels and radio stations. NDTV Hindu was almost on a self-destruct countdown.

In terms of content, I did my best to enliven the news. The team was young, energetic, sincere, and raring to go. We increased news bulletins to seventeen a day, with no repeats or 'chunked' shows as they were called. The focus was on live reports and breaking news. Headlines were made snappy with breathes from catchy sound bites, news beats were assigned with dedicated resources for investigative stories, peppy segments were introduced: 'Scrip Tease', a business section with callers on the stock market; 'Green Signal' –a segment on live traffic updates; 'Bill of Rights', an exclusive show on consumer rights and awareness; and 'Bake a Wish', where viewers could wish their friends and families on their birthdays and the most creative wish would win a cake!

My editorial responsibilities aside, I worked hard on my own shows; 'Chennai Speaks Out', a weekly debate on contentious issues with a studio audience; 'Corridors of Power', a hard-hitting 'walk the talk' show with newsmakers; and 'Voice of Chennai', a programme with viewers calling in or joining us through a live video link and interacting with an official in the studio. I remember a viewer had complained about a fallen tree blocking his gate. By the end of the show, the Corporation Commissioner, who was in the studio with me, had initiated action immediately and the elated viewer went on record to thank the channel and the official. A leading intellectual of the city – environmentalist, historian, author, and Director of the C.P.R. Art Foundation Dr. Nanditha Krishna – had once texted me to say that my shows like 'Chennai Speaks Out' should be on the national network. If wishes were horses, local channels would ride on TRPs!

Campaigns were run. A series of stories to 'Save Our Pavements' was assigned to our Reporter on the civic beat. A child had been missing from the Marina Beach. We started a campaign 'Search For Tamana' by airing her picture on every bulletin with updates on the investigation till the little girl was reunited with her parents. At the Police Commissioner's Office, the girl planted a kiss on Commissioner J.K. Tripathy's cheek and her parents thanked NDTV Hindu and me for the support. My children's paediatrician Dr. Benny Benjamin brought the plight of one of his poor patients, Baby Ganesh, to my attention. The child of an auto driver had fallen into a drainage chamber and suffered brain damage. We ran a campaign 'Save Baby Ganesh' and mobilised funds for his treatment. A family friend and world squash champion Dipika Pallikal came forward to do her bit. We were the only channel to start converting blood donation requests that many of us would get through SMS messages into repeated mentions on the news scroll.

When the Nithyananda 'Sex Scandal' broke, I took a decision not to air those clips as we were a family channel. It adversely affected our ratings that week. Towards the end of 2011, due to the financial dire straits we were in, I even breached the 'Chinese Wall' between Editorial and Marketing and accompanied the Chief Operating Officer and my good friend Pranav Bakshi on sales calls. I managed to get a few friends like Akshaya Homes Founder Chitty Babu to place advertisements and the head of Ceebros Subba Reddy to sponsor our Awards night at his Rain Tree hotel. But obviously this was not enough to fight the inherent drawbacks.

Decency, sensitivity and not following the sensational herd cost us dearly. In the run up to the sale of the channel to the

Thanthi Group (NDTV Hindu morphed into a Tamil channel called Thanthi TV) I received many calls from Corporate head honchos and public figures to say how we would be missed. But none of them put their money where their words were.

The phrase 'Content Is King' is a load of rubbish. It's not 'stuff' but 'fluff' that is the King, Queen and the Kingdom, if you please.

ABOUT THE AUTHOR

BEFORE DONNING THE BLACK gown as an Advocate in the Madras High Court, Sanjay Pinto was a household name in India on the NDTV network for a decade and a half. A former Bureau Chief and Resident Editor of NDTV 24x7 and the Executive Editor of NDTV Hindu, his reports from ground zero in South India are still remembered.

When he is not arguing in court, Sanjay wears other hats – as a Columnist, Political Analyst on prime time TV debates, Public Speaker and Guest Lecturer at Law Schools. Not to forget his role as a doting dad of twin angels and a besotted husband.

A former National Debating Champion from Loyola College & the Dr. Ambedkar Government Law College, he is a recipient of Rotary Awards for his excellence in the Media & Law. This is his third book.

50